The Blessing Bible

"And all these blessings shall come on thee,
and overtake thee, if thou shalt hearken unto
the voice of the Lord thy God."
Deuteronomy 28:2

Unless otherwise indicated, all Scripture quotations are taken from the King James Version of the Bible.

The Blessing Bible
ISBN 1-56394-211-9
Copyright © 1986 by *MIKE MURDOCK*
All publishing rights belong exclusively to Wisdom International
Published by The Wisdom Center
P. O. Box 99 • Denton, Texas 76202
1-888-WISDOM-1 (1-888-947-3661)
Website: thewisdomcenter.cc

A PERSONAL WORD FROM MIKE MURDOCK

―――――▸◗◖◖――――

Dear Partner,

This book was created especially for you.

Your success is so very important to me. God has called and anointed me to help you achieve His dreams and goals in your life...the secret is the Wisdom of His Word.

I have chronologically sequenced these scriptures from Genesis through the Revelation...to create your awareness of the *nature* of your Heavenly Father to bless, benefit and reward *every act of obedience.*

Welcome to God's marvelous Reward System for those who respect Wisdom enough to pursue it.

In Jesus' Love,

MIKE MURDOCK

EXAMPLES OF BLESSINGS

Throughout the Bible, God has blessed His people. For your encouragement, exhortation and inspiration, the following represents actual examples of God's blessings in the lives of real people. These blessings belong to all generations, to all who meet God's conditions (Deut. 7:9).

Adam	Gen. 1:26,29-30	Dominion
Noah	Gen. 9:1,14-15	Fruitfulness
Abraham	Gen. 12:1-3	Favor
Sarah	Gen. 21:1-2	Family
Isaac	Gen. 26:3	Provision
Jacob	Gen. 32:24,26-29	Power
Joseph	Gen. 49:22,25	Fruitfulness
Ephraim	Gen. 48:20	Promotion
Benjamin	Deut. 33:12	Protection
Moses	Deut. 34:10	Fellowship with God
Joshua	Josh. 2:5	Power
Hannah	1 Sam. 1:20	Family
Samuel	1 Sam. 2:26	Favor
David	1 Sam. 16:13	Holy Spirit
Solomon	1 Kings 3:12-13	Understanding
Widow Zarephath	1 Kings 17:13-14	Provision
Hezekiah	2 Kings 20:6	Longevity
Jehoshaphat	2 Chron. 17:5	Abundance
Esther	Esther 2:17	Grace
Job	Job 42:12	Restoration
Cyrus	Isa. 45:2-3	Prosperity
Jeremiah	Jer. 1:9-10	Authority
Daniel	Dan. 6:22	Protection
Zacchaeus	Luke 19:9	Salvation
Cornelius	Acts 10:30-31 (...a man stood...)	Faithfulness of God
Peter	Acts 12:11	Deliverance
Paul	2 Tim. 4:18	Security
Elijah	James 5:18	Power
All Believers	1 John 3:1-2	Heaven

EXAMPLES OF BLESSINGS

ADAM

Genesis 1:26 — And God said, Let us make man in Our image, after Our likeness: and let them have dominion over the fish of the sea, and over the fowl of the air, and over the cattle, and over all the earth, and over every creeping thing that creepeth upon the earth.

Genesis 1:29,30 — And God said, Behold, I have given you every herb bearing Seed, which is upon the face of all the earth, and every tree, in the which is the fruit of a tree yielding Seed; to you it shall be for meat. And to every beast of the earth, and to every fowl of the air, and to every thing that creepeth upon the earth, wherein there is life, I have given every green herb for meat: and it was so.

NOAH

Genesis 9:1 — And God blessed Noah and his sons, and said unto them, Be fruitful, and multiply, and replenish the earth.

Genesis 9:14,15 — And it shall come to pass, when I bring a cloud over the earth, that the bow shall be seen in the cloud: And I will remember My covenant, which is between Me and you and every living creature of all flesh; and the waters shall no more become a flood to destroy all flesh.

ABRAHAM
Genesis 12:1-3 — Now the Lord had said unto Abram, Get thee out of thy country, and from thy kindred, and from thy father's house, unto a land that I will shew thee: And I will make of thee a great nation, and I will bless thee, and make thy name great; and thou shalt be a blessing: And I will bless them that bless thee, and curse him that curseth thee: and in thee shall all families of the earth be blessed.

SARAH
Genesis 21:1,2 — And the Lord visited Sarah as He had said, and the Lord did unto Sarah as He had spoken. For Sarah conceived, and bare Abraham a son in his old age, at the set time of which God had spoken to him.

ISAAC
Genesis 26:3 — Sojourn in this land, and I will be with thee, and will bless thee; for unto thee, and unto thy Seed, I will give all these countries, and I will perform the oath which I sware unto Abraham thy father;

JACOB
Genesis 32:24 — And Jacob was left alone; and there wrestled a man with him until the breaking of the day.

Genesis 32:26-29 — And he said, Let me go, for the day breaketh. And he said, I will not let thee go, except thou bless me. And he said unto him, What is thy name? And he said, Jacob. And he said, Thy name shall be called no more Jacob, but Israel: for as a prince hast thou power with God and with men, and hast prevailed. And Jacob asked him, and said, Tell me, I pray thee, thy name. And he said, Wherefore is it that thou dost ask after my name? And he blessed him there.

JOSEPH
Genesis 49:22 — Joseph is a fruitful bough, even a fruitful bough by a well; whose branches run over the wall:

Genesis 49:25 — Even by the God of thy father, who shall help thee; and by the Almighty, who shall bless thee with blessings of heaven above, blessings of the deep that lieth under, blessings of the breasts, and of the womb:

EPHRAIM
Genesis 48:20 — And He blessed them that day, saying, In thee shall Israel bless, saying, God make thee as Ephraim and as Manasseh: and He set Ephraim before Manasseh.

BENJAMIN
Deuteronomy 33:12 — And of Benjamin He said, The beloved of the Lord shall dwell in safety by Him; and the Lord shall cover him all the day long, and He shall dwell between his shoulders.

MOSES
Deuteronomy 34:10 — And there arose not a prophet since in Israel like unto Moses, whom the Lord knew face to face,

JOSHUA
Joshua 2:5 — And it came to pass about the time of shutting of the gate, when it was dark, that the men went out: whither the men went I wot not: pursue after them quickly; for ye shall overtake them.

HANNAH
1 Samuel 1:20 — Wherefore it came to pass, when the time was come about after Hannah had conceived, that she bare a son, and called his name Samuel, saying, Because I have asked him of the Lord.

SAMUEL
1 Samuel 2:26 — And the child Samuel grew on, and was in favour both with the Lord, and also with men.

DAVID
1 Samuel 16:13 — Then Samuel took the horn of oil, and anointed him in the midst of his brethren: and the spirit of the Lord came upon David from that day forward. So Samuel rose up, and went to Ramah.

SOLOMON
1 Kings 3:12,13 — Behold, I have done according to thy words: lo, I have given thee a wise and an understanding heart; so that there was none like thee before thee, neither after thee shall any arise like unto thee. And I have also given thee that which thou hast not asked, both riches, and honour: so that there shall not be any among the kings like unto thee all thy days.

ZAREPHATH WIDOW

1 Kings 17:13,14 — And Elijah said unto her, Fear not; go and do as thou hast said: but make me thereof a little cake first, and bring it unto me, and after make for thee and for thy son. For thus saith the Lord God of Israel, The barrel of meal shall not waste, neither shall the cruse of oil fail, until the day that the Lord sendeth rain upon the earth.

HEZEKIAH

2 Kings 20:6 — And I will add unto thy days fifteen years; and I will deliver thee and this city out of the hand of the king of Assyria; and I will defend this city for Mine own sake, and for My servant David's sake.

JEHOSHAPHAT

2 Chronicles 17:5 — Therefore the Lord stablished the kingdom in His hand; and all Judah brought to Jehoshaphat presents; and he had riches and honour in abundance.

ESTHER

Esther 2:17 — And the king loved Esther above all the women, and she obtained grace and favour in his sight more than all the virgins; so that he set the royal crown upon her head, and made her queen instead of Vashti.

JOB

Job 42:12 — So the Lord blessed the latter end of Job more than his beginning: for he had fourteen thousand sheep, and six thousand camels, and a thousand yoke of oxen, and a thousand she asses.

CYRUS
Isaiah 45:2,3 — I will go before thee, and make the crooked places straight: I will break in pieces the gates of brass, and cut in sunder the bars of iron: And I will give thee the treasures of darkness, and hidden riches of secret places, that thou mayest know that I, the Lord, which call thee by thy name, am the God of Israel.

JEREMIAH
Jeremiah 1:9,10 — Then the Lord put forth His hand, and touched my mouth. And the Lord said unto me, Behold, I have put My words in thy mouth. See, I have this day set thee over the nations and over the kingdoms, to root out, and to pull down, and to destroy, and to throw down, to build, and to plant.

DANIEL
Daniel 6:22 — My God hath sent His angel, and hath shut the lions' mouths, that they have not hurt me: forasmuch as before Him innocency was found in me; and also before thee, O king, have I done no hurt.

ZACCHAEUS
Luke 19:9 — And Jesus said unto him, This day is salvation come to this house, forsomuch as he also is a son of Abraham.

CORNELIUS
Acts 10:30,31 — ...a man stood before me in bright clothing, And said, Cornelius, thy prayer is heard, and thine alms are had in remembrance in the sight of God.

PETER
Acts 12:11 — And when Peter was come to himself, he said, Now I know of a surety, that the Lord hath sent His angel, and hath delivered me out of the hand of Herod, and from all the expectation of the people of the Jews.

PAUL
2 Timothy 4:18 — And the Lord shall deliver me from every evil work, and will preserve me unto His heavenly kingdom: to Whom be glory for ever and ever. Amen.

ELIJAH
James 5:18 — And he prayed again, and the heaven gave rain, and the earth brought forth her fruit.

ALL BELIEVERS
1 John 3:1,2 — Behold, what manner of love the Father hath bestowed upon us, that we should be called the sons of God: therefore the world knoweth us not, because it knew Him not. Beloved, now are we the sons of God, and it doth not yet appear what we shall be: but we know that, when He shall appear, we shall be like Him; for we shall see Him as He is.

THE BLESSINGS

1. Abilities   Ex. 31:3; Rom. 12:6; 1 Cor. 12:4-7;
2 Cor. 1:4
2. Abundance   Deut. 15:6,7; Deut. 30:9; Ps. 92:12;
Isa. 41:18; Mal. 3:10
3. Angels   Ps. 34:7; Ps. 91:11,12; Isa. 63:9;
Matt. 4:11; Matt. 18:10
4. Assurance   Gen. 26:3; Ezk. 34:16; Jn. 14:18;
Rom. 8:28; Heb. 6:17,18;
Heb. 13:6
5. Authority   Gen. 1:27,28; Gen. 9:2;
2 Sam. 22:30; Lk. 10:19
6. Church   Ps. 122:1; Isa. 54:17; Hag. 2:9;
Rom. 12:5; Eph. 2:19-22
7. Confidence   Isa. 40:31; 2 Cor. 3:5; 2 Cor. 9:8;
Phil. 1:6; 1 Jn. 4:4
8. Deliverance   Ex. 3:8; Ps. 18:19; Ps. 34:9;
Isa. 10:27; 2 Tim. 4:18
9. Eternal Life   Job 19:25,26; Matt. 16:25, 27;
Jn. 3:16; Rom. 6:23; 1 Jn. 5:11;
Rev. 22:5
10. Eternal Honor   Mal. 3:17; James 1:12; 1 Pet. 1:4;
Rev. 2:17; Rev. 3:12,21; Rev. 21:7
11. Faith   Mk. 9:23; Lk. 17:6; Rom. 1:17;
Rom. 5:1,2; Gal. 3:11
12. Faithfulness   Num. 23:19; Deut. 7:9;
of God   1 Kings 8:56; Ps. 121:3,4;
Ps. 145:18,19; Isa. 54:10;
Jn. 6:37; Heb. 13:5

13. Family   Gen. 15:4,5; Gen. 22:17,18;
    Gen. 28:14; Ps. 68:6; Ps. 127:3;
    Acts 16:31

14. Favor   Gen. 12:2; Ps. 5:12; Prov. 3:4;
    Prov. 16:15

15. Fellowship   Song of Sol. 2:3,4; Jer. 29:13;
With God   Matt. 12:50; Jn. 14:23; Rom. 8:17;
    2 Cor. 6:18; Rev. 3:20

16. Forgiveness   Ps. 130:3,4; Is. 43:25; Matt. 6:14;
    Lk. 15:20; 1 Jn. 1:9

17. Freedom   Ps. 46:1,2; Ps. 56:3,4,9;
from Fear   Ps. 118:6; 2 Thess. 3:3; 2 Tim. 1:7

18. Freedom   Ps. 3:5,6; Ps. 55:22; Matt. 6:34;
from Worry   Jn. 14:27; Rev. 1:17,18

19. Friendship   Prov. 18:24; Isa. 41:8; Jn. 15:13,14

20. Fruitfulness   Ps. 92:14; Zech. 8:12; Gal. 5:22

21. Grace   Ps. 103:12,13; Isa. 53:5; Rom. 5:20;
    2 Cor. 12:9; Eph. 2:8

22. Guidance   Ps. 25:9; Ps. 32:8; Ps. 73:23-25;
    Ps. 139:10,11; Prov. 3:6; Is. 30:21;
    Is. 49:10

23. Happiness   Ps. 37:4,5; Ps. 63:4,5; Ps. 64:10;
    Ps. 84:11; Jn. 10:10; Jn. 13:17

24. Health   Ex. 15:26; Ps. 103:2,3; Ps. 147:3;
    Jer. 30:17; Matt. 9:35

25. Heaven   Dan. 12:3; Mk. 14:25; Jn. 14:2;
    1 Cor. 2:9; 1 Cor. 13:12; Rev. 21:3,4

26. Holy Spirit   Lk. 11:13; Jn. 7:38; Jn. 14:26;
    Jn. 16:13; 1 Cor. 2:10,11

27. Hope   Ps. 71:5; Rom. 5:4,5; Rom. 8:24;
    Rom. 15:13; Heb. 6:19.28.

28. Inspiration   Job 32:8; Prov. 20:27; Lk. 12:12;
    Phil. 4:8

29. Intercession   Isa. 53:12; Jn. 17:15; Rom. 8:27;
James 5:16

30. Joy   Neh. 8:10; Ps. 3:3; Ps. 16:11;
Ps. 30:5; Ps. 118:24; Ps. 126:5,6;
Isa. 12:3; Isa. 51:11

31. Justice   Ps. 72:4; Ps. 89:14; Isa. 33:22;
1 Cor. 4:4

32. Knowledge   2 Chron. 1:12; Prov. 9:10; Isa. 33:6;
Matt. 10:19

33. Longevity   Deut. 4:9; Deut. 11:21; Job 5:26;
Ps. 21:4; Ps. 91:16;
Prov. 3:1,2; Prov. 9:11

34. Love   Jn. 15:10; Rom. 8:38,39;
1 Jn. 4:10

35. Marriage   Gen. 2:24; Ps. 128:3; Prov. 18:22;
Prov. 31:11,12; 1 Cor. 7:14

36. Mercy   Gen. 9:16; Gen. 39:21; Ex. 33:19;
Deut. 4:31; Ps. 36:5; Ps. 86:5,7;
Ps. 145:8,9; Matt. 10:42

37. Miracles   Ex. 14:27-30; Ps. 105:39,40;
Matt. 19:26

38. Ministry   Isa. 61:1; Jn. 15:16; Rom. 10:15;
1 Pet. 2:9

39. Peace   Lev. 26:6; Ps. 29:11; Ps. 72:7;
Isa. 26:3; Is. 54:13; Phil. 4:7;
2 Thess. 3:16

40. Power   Ex. 9:16; Deut. 4:37; Deut. 11:25;
Ps. 44:5,7; Isa. 59:19;
Matt. 10:1,8; Jn. 14:12; Acts 1:8

41. Promotion   Deut. 1:10; Deut. 28:13;
1 Sam 2:8; Ps. 71:21;
Matt. 5:5; Matt. 23:12;
Eph. 2:6; James 4:10; 1 Pet. 5:6

42. Prosperity   Gen. 13:14,15; Lev. 20:24;
                  Lev. 26:9; 2 Chron. 26:5;
                  Ps. 35:27; 3 Jn. 1:2
43. Protection   Gen. 15:1; Deut. 1:30;
                  2 Chron. 20:15; Ps. 27:5;
                  Ps. 91:2-7; Isa. 43:2; Nah. 1:7;
                  Lk. 12:7
44. Provision   Deut. 8:7-9; Deut. 28:3-5;
                  1 Kings 17:14; Ps. 37:3,25;
                  Ps. 68:19; Ps. 145:15,16
45. Rest   Ps. 4:8; Ps. 23:2; Prov. 1:33;
                  Prov. 3:24; Is. 14:3;
                  Jer. 30:10; Matt. 11:28,29
46. Restoration   Lev. 26:13; Job 42:10;
                  Ps. 20:8; Ps. 23:3; Ps. 40:2,3;
                  Ps. 103:5; Ps. 138:3,7; 2 Cor. 5:17
47. Resurrection Isa. 25:8; Jn. 5:21; Jn. 11:25,26;
                  Rom. 6:5; Rom. 8:11
48. Riches   Deut. 8:18; 1 Chron. 29:12;
                  Prov. 8:18,19; Prov. 22:4;
                  Eccl. 5:19; Isa. 45:3; 2 Cor. 8:9
49. Salvation   Ps. 27:1; Ps. 55:16;
                  Jn. 6:54; Rom. 1:16; Rom. 5:7,8;
                  Col. 1:14
50. Security   Ps. 26:1; Ps. 57:3; Ps. 62:2,7,8;
                  Ps. 105:14,15; Jer. 17:8; Matt. 7:25
51. Strength   Josh. 23:9; 1 Chron. 16:27;
                  Ps. 18:2,29,32; Ps. 125:1;
                  Isa. 40:29
52. Success   Josh. 1:8; Isa. 58:11; Phil. 4:19
53. Truth   Mark 4:22; Jn. 8:32; Jn. 14:6;
                  Jn. 17:19; 2 Jn. 1:2

54. Understanding1 Kings 3:12; Ps. 111:10;
                Ps. 119:130; Prov. 2:11;
                Lk. 24:45; Eph. 1:18; 2 Tim. 2:7
55. Victory   Ps. 60:12; Ps. 108:13;
                Eph. 6:13-17; 1 Jn. 5:4
56. Wisdom   1 Kings 4:29; Prov. 2:6,7;
                Lk. 21:15; James 1:5
57. Word of God Ps. 19:7,8; Ps. 107:20;
                Ps. 119:1,2,9,45,50;
                Isa. 55:11; Jer. 15:16
58. Work   Deut. 15:10; Deut. 28:2,12;
                Ps. 1:3; Eccl. 3:13

BOOKS OF THE BIBLE

OLD TESTAMENT

Genesis
Exodus
Leviticus
Numbers
Deuteronomy
Joshua
Judges
Ruth
1 Samuel
2 Samuel
1 Kings
2 Kings
1 Chronicles

2 Chronicles
Ezra
Nehemiah
Esther
Job
Psalm
Proverbs
Ecclesiastes
Song of Solomon
Isaiah
Jeremiah
Lamentations
Ezekiel

Daniel
Hosea
Joel
Amos
Obediah
Jonah
Micah
Nahum
Habakkuk
Zephaniah
Haggai
Zechariah
Malachi

NEW TESTAMENT

Matthew
Mark
Luke
John
Acts
Romans
1 Corinthians
2 Corinthians
Galatians
Ephesians
Philippians
Colossians
1 Thessalonians
2 Thessalonians

1 Timothy
2 Timothy
Titus
Philemon
Hebrews
James
1 Peter
2 Peter
1 John
2 John
3 John
Jude
Revelation

THE BLESSINGS...
OLD TESTAMENT

GENESIS

CHAPTER 1

26) And God said, Let us make man in Our image, after Our likeness: and let them have dominion over the fish of the sea, and over the fowl of the air, and over the cattle, and over all the earth, and over every creeping thing that creepeth upon the earth.

27) So God created man in His own image, in the image of God created He him; male and female created He them.

28) And God blessed them, and God said unto them, Be fruitful, and multiply, and replenish the earth, and subdue it: and have dominion over the fish of the sea, and over the fowl of the air, and over every living thing that moveth upon the earth.

29) And God said, Behold, I have given you every herb bearing Seed, which is upon the face of all the earth, and every tree, in the which is the fruit of a tree yielding Seed; to you it shall be for meat.

30) And to every beast of the earth, and to every fowl of the air, and to every thing that creepeth upon the earth, wherein there is life, I have given every green herb for meat: and it was so.

31) And God saw every thing that He had made, and, behold, it was very good. And the evening and the morning were the sixth day.

CHAPTER 2

18) And the Lord God said, It is not good that the man should be alone; I will make him an help meet for him.

24) Therefore shall a man leave his father and his mother, and shall cleave unto his wife: and they shall be one flesh.

CHAPTER 9

1) And God blessed Noah and his sons, and said unto them, Be fruitful, and multiply, and replenish the earth.

2) And the fear of you and the dread of you shall be upon every beast of the earth, and upon every fowl of the air, upon all that moveth upon the earth, and upon all the fishes of the sea; into your hand are they delivered.

7) And you, be ye fruitful, and multiply; bring forth abundantly in the earth, and multiply therein.

8) And God spake unto Noah, and to his sons with him, saying,

9) And I, behold, I establish My covenant with you, and with your Seed after you;

10) And with every living creature that is with you, of the fowl, of the cattle, and of every beast of the earth with you; from all that go out of the ark, to every beast of the earth.

11) And I will establish My covenant with you; neither shall all flesh be cut off any more by the waters of a flood; neither shall there any more be a flood to destroy the earth.

12) And God said, This is the token of the covenant which I make between Me and you and every living creature that is with you, for perpetual generations:

13) I do set My bow in the cloud, and it shall be for a token of a covenant between Me and the earth.

14) And it shall come to pass, when I bring a cloud over the earth, that the bow shall be seen in the cloud:

15) And I will remember My covenant, which is between Me and you and every living creature of all flesh; and the waters shall no more become a flood to destroy all flesh.

16) And the bow shall be in the cloud; and I will look upon it, that I may remember the everlasting covenant between God and every living creature of all flesh that is upon the earth.

17) And God said unto Noah, This is the token of the covenant, which I have established between Me and all flesh that is upon the earth.

CHAPTER 12

1)   Now the Lord had said unto Abram, Get thee out of thy country, and from thy kindred, and from thy father's house, unto a land that I will shew thee:

2)   And I will make of thee a great nation, and I will bless thee, and make thy name great; and thou shalt be a blessing:

3)   And I will bless them that bless thee, and curse him that curseth thee: and in thee shall all families of the earth be blessed.

CHAPTER 13

14) And the Lord said unto Abram, after that Lot was separated from Him, Lift up now thine eyes, and look from the place where thou art northward, and southward, and eastward, and westward:

15) For all the land which thou seest, to thee will I give it, and to thy Seed for ever.

16) And I will make thy Seed as the dust of the earth: so that if a man can number the dust of the earth, then shall thy Seed also be numbered.

17) Arise, walk through the land in the length of it and in the breadth of it; for I will give it unto thee.

CHAPTER 15

1) After these things the word of the Lord came unto Abram in a vision, saying, Fear not, Abram: I am thy shield, and thy exceeding great reward.

4) And, behold, the word of the Lord came unto him, saying, This shall not be thine heir; but he that shall come forth out of thine own bowels shall be thine heir.

5) And He brought him forth abroad, and said, Look now toward Heaven, and tell the stars, if thou be able to number them: and He said unto him, So shall thy Seed be.

6) And he believed in the Lord; and He counted it to him for righteousness.

CHAPTER 17

1) And when Abram was ninety years old and nine, the Lord appeared to Abram, and said unto him, I am the Almighty God; walk before Me, and be thou perfect.

2) And I will make My covenant between Me and thee, and will multiply thee exceedingly.

6) And I will make thee exceeding fruitful, and I will make nations of thee, and kings shall come out of thee.

7) And I will establish My covenant between

Me and thee and thy Seed after thee in their generations for an everlasting covenant, to be a God unto thee, and to thy Seed after thee.

CHAPTER 22

17) That in blessing I will bless thee, and in multiplying I will multiply thy Seed as the stars of the Heaven, and as the sand which is upon the sea shore; and thy Seed shall possess the gate of his enemies;

18) And in thy Seed shall all the nations of the earth be blessed; because thou hast obeyed My voice.

CHAPTER 26

3) Sojourn in this land, and I will be with thee, and will bless thee; for unto thee, and unto thy Seed, I will give all these countries, and I will perform the oath which I sware unto Abraham thy father;

4) And I will make thy Seed to multiply as the stars of Heaven, and will give unto thy Seed all these countries; and in thy Seed shall all the nations of the earth be blessed;

12) Then Isaac sowed in that land, and received in the same year an hundredfold: and the Lord blessed him.

13) And the man waxed great, and went forward, and grew until he became very great:

14) For he had possession of flocks, and possession of herds, and great store of servants: and the Philistines envied him.

CHAPTER 28

13) And, behold, the Lord stood above it, and said, I am the Lord God of Abraham thy father, and the God of Isaac: the land whereon thou liest, to thee will I give it, and to thy Seed;

14) And thy Seed shall be as the dust of the earth, and thou shalt spread abroad to the west, and to the east, and to the north, and to the south: and in thee and in thy Seed shall all the families of the earth be blessed.

15) And, behold, I am with thee, and will keep thee in all places whither thou goest, and will bring thee again into this land; for I will not leave thee, until I have done that which I have spoken to thee of.

CHAPTER 39

2) And the Lord was with Joseph, and he was a prosperous man; and he was in the house of his master the Egyptian.

3) And his master saw that the Lord was with him, and that the Lord made all that he did to prosper in his hand.

4) And Joseph found grace in his sight, and he served him: and he made him overseer over his house, and all that he had he put into his hand.

5) And it came to pass from the time that he had made him overseer in his house, and over all that he had, that the Lord blessed the Egyptian's house for Joseph's sake; and the blessing of the Lord was upon all that he had in the house, and in the field.

6) And he left all that he had in Joseph's hand;

and he knew not ought he had, save the bread which he did eat. And Joseph was a goodly person, and well favoured.

20) And Joseph's master took him, and put him into the prison, a place where the king's prisoners were bound: and he was there in the prison.

21) But the Lord was with Joseph, and shewed him mercy, and gave him favour in the sight of the keeper of the prison.

22) And the keeper of the prison committed to Joseph's hand all the prisoners that were in the prison; and whatsoever they did there, he was the doer of it.

23) The keeper of the prison looked not to any thing that was under his hand; because the Lord was with him, and that which he did, the Lord made it to prosper.

CHAPTER 45

7)   And God sent me before you to preserve you a posterity in the earth, and to save your lives by a great deliverance.

CHAPTER 49

25) Even by the God of thy father, who shall help thee; and by the Almighty, who shall bless thee with blessings of Heaven above, blessings of the deep that lieth under, blessings of the breasts, and of the womb:

26) The blessings of thy father have prevailed above the blessings of my progenitors unto the utmost bound of the everlasting hills: they shall be on the head of Joseph, and on the crown of the head of him that was separate from his brethren.

EXODUS

CHAPTER 1

20) Therefore God dealt well with the midwives: and the people multiplied, and waxed very mighty.

21) And it came to pass, because the midwives feared God, that He made them houses.

CHAPTER 2

23) And it came to pass in process of time, that the king of Egypt died: and the children of Israel sighed by reason of the bondage, and they cried, and their cry came up unto God by reason of the bondage.

24) And God heard their groaning, and God remembered His covenant with Abraham, with Isaac, and with Jacob.

25) And God looked upon the children of Israel, and God had respect unto them.

CHAPTER 3

7) And the Lord said, I have surely seen the affliction of My people which are in Egypt, and have heard their cry by reason of their taskmasters; for I know their sorrows;

8) And I am come down to deliver them out of the hand of the Egyptians, and to bring them up out of that land unto a good land and a large, unto a land flowing with milk and honey; unto the place of the Canaanites, and the Hittites, and the Amorites, and the Perizzites, and the Hivites, and the Jebusites.

9) Now therefore, behold, the cry of the children of Israel is come unto Me: and I have also seen the

oppression wherewith the Egyptians oppress them.

CHAPTER 6

6)   Wherefore say unto the children of Israel, I am the Lord, and I will bring you out from under the burdens of the Egyptians, and I will rid you out of their bondage, and I will redeem you with a stretched out arm, and with great judgments:

7)   And I will take you to Me for a people, and I will be to you a God: and ye shall know that I am the Lord your God, which bringeth you out from under the burdens of the Egyptians.

8)   And I will bring you in unto the land, concerning the which I did swear to give it to Abraham, to Isaac, and to Jacob; and I will give it you for an heritage: I am the Lord.

CHAPTER 9

16)   And in very deed for this cause have I raised thee up, for to shew in thee My power; and that My name may be declared throughout all the earth.

CHAPTER 14

13)   And Moses said unto the people, Fear ye not, stand still, and see the salvation of the Lord, which He will shew to you to day: for the Egyptians whom ye have seen to day, ye shall see them again no more for ever.

14)   The Lord shall fight for you, and ye shall hold your peace.

26)   And the Lord said unto Moses, Stretch out thine hand over the sea, that the waters may come

again upon the Egyptians, upon their chariots, and upon their horsemen.

27) And Moses stretched forth his hand over the sea, and the sea returned to his strength when the morning appeared; and the Egyptians fled against it; and the Lord overthrew the Egyptians in the midst of the sea.

28) And the waters returned, and covered the chariots, and the horsemen, and all the host of Pharaoh that came into the sea after them; there remained not so much as one of them.

29) But the children of Israel walked upon dry land in the midst of the sea; and the waters were a wall unto them on their right hand, and on their left.

30) Thus the Lord saved Israel that day out of the hand of the Egyptians; and Israel saw the Egyptians dead upon the sea shore.

CHAPTER 15

2) The Lord is my strength and song, and He is become my salvation: He is my God, and I will prepare Him an habitation; my father's God, and I will exalt Him.

26) And said, If thou wilt diligently hearken to the voice of the Lord thy God, and wilt do that which is right in His sight, and wilt give ear to His commandments, and keep all His statutes, I will put none of these diseases upon thee, which I have brought upon the Egyptians: for I am the Lord that healeth thee.

CHAPTER 23

19) The first of the firstfruits of thy land thou

shalt bring into the house of the Lord thy God. Thou shalt not seethe a kid in his mother's milk.

20)   Behold, I send an Angel before thee, to keep thee in the way, and to bring thee into the place which I have prepared.

22)   But if thou shalt indeed obey his voice, and do all that I speak; then I will be an enemy unto thine enemies, and an adversary unto thine adversaries.

25)   And ye shall serve the Lord your God, and He shall bless thy bread, and thy water; and I will take sickness away from the midst of thee.

26)   There shall nothing cast their young, nor be barren, in thy land: the number of thy days I will fulfil.

27)   I will send My fear before thee, and will destroy all the people to whom thou shalt come, and I will make all thine enemies turn their backs unto thee.

30)   By little and little I will drive them out from before thee, until thou be increased, and inherit the land.

CHAPTER 31

3)   And I have filled him with the Spirit of God, in Wisdom, and in understanding, and in knowledge, and in all manner of workmanship,

CHAPTER 33

14)   And He said, My presence shall go with thee, and I will give thee rest.

19)   And He said, I will make all My goodness pass before thee, and I will proclaim the name of the

Lord before thee; and will be gracious to whom I will be gracious, and will shew mercy on whom I will shew mercy.

LEVITICUS

CHAPTER 20

22) Ye shall therefore keep all My statutes, and all My judgments, and do them: that the land, whither I bring you to dwell therein, spue you not out.

24) But I have said unto you, Ye shall inherit their land, and I will give it unto you to possess it, a land that floweth with milk and honey: I am the Lord your God, which have separated you from other people.

CHAPTER 26

3)   If ye walk in My statutes, and keep My commandments, and do them;

4)   Then I will give you rain in due season, and the land shall yield her increase, and the trees of the field shall yield their fruit.

5)   And your threshing shall reach unto the vintage, and the vintage shall reach unto the sowing time: and ye shall eat your bread to the full, and dwell in your land safely.

6)   And I will give peace in the land, and ye shall lie down, and none shall make you afraid: and I will rid evil beasts out of the land, neither shall the sword go through your land.

7)   And ye shall chase your enemies, and they

shall fall before you by the sword.

8)   And five of you shall chase an hundred, and an hundred of you shall put ten thousand to flight: and your enemies shall fall before you by the sword.

9)   For I will have respect unto you, and make you fruitful, and multiply you, and establish My covenant with you.

10)   And ye shall eat old store, and bring forth the old because of the new.

11)   And I will set My tabernacle among you: and My soul shall not abhor you.

12)   And I will walk among you, and will be your God, and ye shall be My people.

13)   I am the Lord your God, which brought you forth out of the land of Egypt, that ye should not be their bondmen; and I have broken the bands of your yoke, and made you go upright.

NUMBERS

CHAPTER 12

6)   And He said, Hear now My words: If there be a prophet among you, I the Lord will make Myself known unto him in a vision, and will speak unto him in a dream.

CHAPTER 14

20)   And the Lord said, I have pardoned according to thy word:

21)   But as truly as I live, all the earth shall be filled with the glory of the Lord.

24)   But My servant Caleb, because he had

another spirit with him, and hath followed Me fully, him will I bring into the land whereinto he went; and his Seed shall possess it.

CHAPTER 23

19) God is not a man, that He should lie; neither the son of man, that He should repent: hath He said, and shall He not do it? or hath He spoken, and shall He not make it good?

DEUTERONOMY

CHAPTER 1

10) The Lord your God hath multiplied you, and, behold, ye are this day as the stars of Heaven for multitude.

30) The Lord your God which goeth before you, He shall fight for you, according to all that He did for you in Egypt before your eyes;

CHAPTER 3

22) Ye shall not fear them: for the Lord your God He shall fight for you.

24) O Lord God, Thou hast begun to shew Thy servant Thy greatness, and Thy mighty hand: for what God is there in Heaven or in earth, that can do according to Thy works, and according to Thy might?

CHAPTER 4

9) Only take heed to thyself, and keep thy soul diligently, lest thou forget the things which thine eyes have seen, and lest they depart from thy heart all

the days of thy life: but teach them thy sons, and thy sons' sons;

29) But if from thence thou shalt seek the Lord thy God, thou shalt find Him, if thou seek Him with all thy heart and with all thy soul.

30) When thou art in tribulation, and all these things are come upon thee, even in the latter days, if thou turn to the Lord thy God, and shalt be obedient unto His voice;

31) (For the Lord thy God is a merciful God;) He will not forsake thee, neither destroy thee, nor forget the covenant of thy fathers which He sware unto them.

34) Or hath God assayed to go and take Him a nation from the midst of another nation, by temptations, by signs, and by wonders, and by war, and by a mighty hand, and by a stretched out arm, and by great terrors, according to all that the Lord your God did for you in Egypt before your eyes?

35) Unto thee it was shewed, that thou mightest know that the Lord He is God; there is none else beside Him.

36) Out of Heaven He made thee to hear His voice, that He might instruct thee: and upon earth He shewed thee His great fire; and thou heardest His words out of the midst of the fire.

37) And because He loved thy fathers, therefore He chose their Seed after them, and brought thee out in His sight with His mighty power out of Egypt;

38) To drive out nations from before thee greater and mightier than thou art, to bring thee in, to give thee their land for an inheritance, as it is this day.

39) Know therefore this day, and consider it in

thine heart, that the Lord He is God in Heaven above, and upon the earth beneath: there is none else.

40) Thou shalt keep therefore His statutes, and His commandments, which I command thee this day, that it may go well with thee, and with thy children after thee, and that thou mayest prolong thy days upon the earth, which the Lord thy God giveth thee, for ever.

CHAPTER 5

31) But as for thee, stand thou here by Me, and I will speak unto thee all the commandments, and the statutes, and the judgments, which thou shalt teach them, that they may do them in the land which I give them to possess it.

32) Ye shall observe to do therefore as the Lord your God hath commanded you: ye shall not turn aside to the right hand or to the left.

33) Ye shall walk in all the ways which the Lord your God hath commanded you, that ye may live, and that it may be well with you, and that ye may prolong your days in the land which ye shall possess.

CHAPTER 6

1) Now these are the commandments, the statutes, and the judgments, which the Lord your God commanded to teach you, that ye might do them in the land whither ye go to possess it:

2) That thou mightest fear the Lord thy God, to keep all His statutes and His commandments, which I command thee, thou, and thy son, and thy son's son, all the days of thy life; and that thy days may be prolonged.

3)   Hear therefore, O Israel, and observe to do it; that it may be well with thee, and that ye may increase mightily, as the Lord God of thy fathers hath promised thee, in the land that floweth with milk and honey.

5)   And thou shalt love the Lord thy God with all thine heart, and with all thy soul, and with all thy might.

6)   And these words, which I command thee this day, shall be in thine heart:

7)   And thou shalt teach them diligently unto thy children, and shalt talk of them when thou sittest in thine house, and when thou walkest by the way, and when thou liest down, and when thou risest up.

8)   And thou shalt bind them for a sign upon thine hand, and they shall be as frontlets between thine eyes.

9)   And thou shalt write them upon the posts of thy house, and on thy gates.

10)   And it shall be, when the Lord thy God shall have brought thee into the land which He sware unto thy fathers, to Abraham, to Isaac, and to Jacob, to give thee great and goodly cities, which thou buildedst not,

11)   And houses full of all good things, which thou filledst not, and wells digged, which thou diggedst not, vineyards and olive trees, which thou plantedst not; when thou shalt have eaten and be full;

17)   Ye shall diligently keep the commandments of the Lord your God, and His testimonies, and His statutes, which He hath commanded thee.

18)   And thou shalt do that which is right and good in the sight of the Lord: that it may be well

with thee, and that thou mayest go in and possess the good land which the Lord sware unto thy fathers,

19) To cast out all thine enemies from before thee, as the Lord hath spoken.

20) And when thy son asketh thee in time to come, saying, What mean the testimonies, and the statutes, and the judgments, which the Lord our God hath commanded you?

21) Then thou shalt say unto thy son, We were Pharaoh's bondmen in Egypt; and the Lord brought us out of Egypt with a mighty hand:

22) And the Lord shewed signs and wonders, great and sore, upon Egypt, upon Pharaoh, and upon all his household, before our eyes:

23) And He brought us out from thence, that He might bring us in, to give us the land which He sware unto our fathers.

24) And the Lord commanded us to do all these statutes, to fear the Lord our God, for our good always, that He might preserve us alive, as it is at this day.

25) And it shall be our righteousness, if we observe to do all these commandments before the Lord our God, as He hath commanded us.

CHAPTER 7

9) Know therefore that the Lord thy God, He is God, the faithful God, which keepeth covenant and mercy with them that love Him and keep His commandments to a thousand generations;

10) And repayeth them that hate Him to their face, to destroy them: He will not be slack to him that hateth Him, He will repay him to his face.

11) Thou shalt therefore keep the commandments, and the statutes, and the judgments, which I command thee this day, to do them.

12) Wherefore it shall come to pass, if ye hearken to these judgments, and keep, and do them, that the Lord thy God shall keep unto thee the covenant and the mercy which He sware unto thy fathers:

13) And He will love thee, and bless thee, and multiply thee: He will also bless the fruit of thy womb, and the fruit of thy land, thy corn, and thy wine, and thine oil, the increase of thy kine, and the flocks of thy sheep, in the land which He sware unto thy fathers to give thee.

14) Thou shalt be blessed above all people: there shall not be male or female barren among you, or among your cattle.

15) And the Lord will take away from thee all sickness, and will put none of the evil diseases of Egypt, which thou knowest, upon thee; but will lay them upon all them that hate thee.

16) And thou shalt consume all the people which the Lord thy God shall deliver thee; thine eye shall have no pity upon them: neither shalt thou serve their gods; for that will be a snare unto thee.

17) If thou shalt say in thine heart, These nations are more than I; how can I dispossess them?

18) Thou shalt not be afraid of them: but shalt well remember what the Lord thy God did unto Pharaoh, and unto all Egypt;

19) The great temptations which thine eyes saw, and the signs, and the wonders, and the mighty hand, and the stretched out arm, whereby the Lord thy

God brought thee out: so shall the Lord thy God do unto all the people of whom thou art afraid.

20) Moreover the Lord thy God will send the hornet among them, until they that are left, and hide themselves from thee, be destroyed.

21) Thou shalt not be affrighted at them: for the Lord thy God is among you, a mighty God and terrible.

22) And the Lord thy God will put out those nations before thee by little and little: thou mayest not consume them at once, lest the beasts of the field increase upon thee.

23) But the Lord thy God shall deliver them unto thee, and shall destroy them with a mighty destruction, until they be destroyed.

24) And He shall deliver their kings into thine hand, and thou shalt destroy their name from under Heaven: there shall no man be able to stand before thee, until thou have destroyed them.

CHAPTER 8

1) All the commandments which I command thee this day shall ye observe to do, that ye may live, and multiply, and go in and possess the land which the Lord sware unto your father.

2) And thou shalt remember all the way which the Lord thy God led thee these forty years in the wilderness, to humble thee, and to prove thee, to know what was in thine heart, whether thou wouldest keep His commandments, or no.

3) And He humbled thee, and suffered thee to hunger, and fed thee with manna, which thou knewest not, neither did thy fathers know; that He

might make thee know that man doth not live by bread only, but by every word that proceedeth out of the mouth of the Lord doth man live.

4)   Thy raiment waxed not old upon thee, neither did thy foot swell, these forty years.

5)   Thou shalt also consider in thine heart, that, as a man chasteneth his son, so the Lord thy God chasteneth thee.

6) Therefore   thou   shalt   keep   the commandments of the Lord thy God, to walk in His ways, and to fear Him.

7)   For the Lord thy God bringeth thee into a good land, a land of brooks of water, of fountains and depths that spring out of valleys and hills;

8)   A land of wheat, and barley, and vines, and fig trees, and pomegranates; a land of oil olive, and honey;

9)   A land wherein thou shalt eat bread without scarceness, thou shalt not lack any thing in it; a land whose stones are iron, and out of whose hills thou mayest dig brass.

10)   When thou hast eaten and art full, then thou shalt bless the Lord thy God for the good land which He hath given thee.

11)   Beware that thou forget not the Lord thy God, in not keeping His commandments, and His judgments, and His statutes, which I command thee this day:

12)   Lest when thou hast eaten and art full, and hast built goodly houses, and dwelt therein;

13)   And when thy herds and thy flocks multiply, and thy silver and thy gold is multiplied, and all that thou hast is multiplied;

14) Then thine heart be lifted up, and thou forget the Lord thy God, which brought thee forth out of the land of Egypt, from the house of bondage;

15) Who led thee through that great and terrible wilderness, wherein were fiery serpents, and scorpions, and drought, where there was no water; who brought thee forth water out of the rock of flint;

16) Who fed thee in the wilderness with manna, which thy fathers knew not, that He might humble thee, and that He might prove thee, to do thee good at thy latter end;

17) And thou say in thine heart, My power and the might of mine hand hath gotten me this wealth.

18) But thou shalt remember the Lord thy God: for it is He that giveth thee power to get wealth, that He may establish His covenant which He sware unto thy fathers, as it is this day.

19) And it shall be, if thou do at all forget the Lord thy God, and walk after other gods, and serve them, and worship them, I testify against you this day that ye shall surely perish.

20) As the nations which the Lord destroyeth before your face, so shall ye perish; because ye would not be obedient unto the voice of the Lord your God.

CHAPTER 11

8) Therefore shall ye keep all the commandments which I command you this day, that ye may be strong, and go in and possess the land, whither ye go to possess it;

9) And that ye may prolong your days in the land, which the Lord sware unto your fathers to give unto them and to their Seed, a land that floweth with

milk and honey.

10) For the land, whither thou goest in to possess it, is not as the land of Egypt, from whence ye came out, where thou sowedst thy Seed, and wateredst it with thy foot, as a garden of herbs:

11) But the land, whither ye go to possess it, is a land of hills and valleys, and drinketh water of the rain of Heaven:

12) A land which the Lord thy God careth for: the eyes of the Lord thy God are always upon it, from the beginning of the year even unto the end of the year.

13) And it shall come to pass, if ye shall hearken diligently unto my commandments which I command you this day, to love the Lord your God, and to serve Him with all your heart and with all your soul,

14) That I will give you the rain of your land in his due season, the first rain and the latter rain, that thou mayest gather in thy corn, and thy wine, and thine oil.

15) And I will send grass in thy fields for thy cattle, that thou mayest eat and be full.

18) Therefore shall ye lay up these My words in your heart and in your soul, and bind them for a sign upon your hand, that they may be as frontlets between your eyes.

19) And ye shall teach them your children, speaking of them when thou sittest in thine house, and when thou walkest by the way, when thou liest down, and when thou risest up.

20) And thou shalt write them upon the door posts of thine house, and upon thy gates:

21) That your days may be multiplied, and the

days of your children, in the land which the Lord sware unto your fathers to give them, as the days of Heaven upon the earth.

22) For if ye shall diligently keep all these commandments which I command you, to do them, to love the Lord your God, to walk in all His ways, and to cleave unto Him;

23) Then will the Lord drive out all these nations from before you, and ye shall possess greater nations and mightier than yourselves.

24) Every place whereon the soles of your feet shall tread shall be yours: from the wilderness and Lebanon, from the river, the river Euphrates, even unto the uttermost sea shall your coast be.

25) There shall no man be able to stand before you: for the Lord your God shall lay the fear of you and the dread of you upon all the land that ye shall tread upon, as He hath said unto you.

26) Behold, I set before you this day a blessing and a curse;

27) A blessing, if ye obey the commandments of the Lord your God, which I command you this day:

28) And a curse, if ye will not obey the commandments of the Lord your God, but turn aside out of the way which I command you this day, to go after other gods, which ye have not known.

CHAPTER 15

1) At the end of every seven years thou shalt make a release.

2) And this is the manner of the release: Every creditor that lendeth ought unto his neighbour shall release it; he shall not exact it of his neighbour, or of

his brother; because it is called the Lord's release.

3)   Of a foreigner thou mayest exact it again: but that which is thine with thy brother thine hand shall release;

4)   Save when there shall be no poor among you; for the Lord shall greatly bless thee in the land which the Lord thy God giveth thee for an inheritance to possess it:

5)   Only if thou carefully hearken unto the voice of the Lord thy God, to observe to do all these commandments which I command thee this day.

6)   For the Lord thy God blesseth thee, as He promised thee: and thou shalt lend unto many nations, but thou shalt not borrow; and thou shalt reign over many nations, but they shall not reign over thee.

7)   If there be among you a poor man of one of thy brethren within any of thy gates in thy land which the Lord thy God giveth thee, thou shalt not harden thine heart, nor shut thine hand from thy poor brother:

8)   But thou shalt open thine hand wide unto him, and shalt surely lend him sufficient for his need, in that which he wanteth.

9)   Beware that there be not a thought in thy wicked heart, saying, The seventh year, the year of release, is at hand; and thine eye be evil against thy poor brother, and thou givest him nought; and he cry unto the Lord against thee, and it be sin unto thee.

10) Thou shalt surely give him, and thine heart shall not be grieved when thou givest unto him: because that for this thing the Lord thy God shall

bless thee in all thy works, and in all that thou puttest thine hand unto.

11) For the poor shall never cease out of the land: therefore I command thee, saying, Thou shalt open thine hand wide unto thy brother, to thy poor, and to thy needy, in thy land.

12) And if thy brother, an Hebrew man, or an Hebrew woman, be sold unto thee, and serve thee six years; then in the seventh year thou shalt let him go free from thee.

13) And when thou sendest him out free from thee, thou shalt not let him go away empty:

14) Thou shalt furnish him liberally out of thy flock, and out of thy floor, and out of thy winepress: of that wherewith the Lord thy God hath blessed thee thou shalt give unto Him.

15) And thou shalt remember that thou wast a bondman in the land of Egypt, and the Lord thy God redeemed thee: therefore I command thee this thing to day.

16) And it shall be, if He say unto thee, I will not go away from thee; because He loveth thee and thine house, because He is well with thee;

CHAPTER 26

15) Look down from Thy holy habitation, from Heaven, and bless Thy people Israel, and the land which Thou hast given us, as Thou swarest unto our fathers, a land that floweth with milk and honey.

16) This day the Lord thy God hath commanded thee to do these statutes and judgments: thou shalt therefore keep and do them with all thine heart, and with all thy soul.

17) Thou hast avouched the Lord this day to be thy God, and to walk in His ways, and to keep His statutes, and His commandments, and His judgments, and to hearken unto His voice:

18) And the Lord hath avouched thee this day to be His peculiar people, as He hath promised thee, and that thou shouldest keep all His commandments;

19) And to make thee high above all nations which He hath made, in praise, and in name, and in honour; and that thou mayest be an holy people unto the Lord thy God, as He hath spoken.

CHAPTER 28

1) And it shall come to pass, if thou shalt hearken diligently unto the voice of the Lord thy God, to observe and to do all His commandments which I command thee this day, that the Lord thy God will set thee on high above all nations of the earth:

2) And all these blessings shall come on thee, and overtake thee, if thou shalt hearken unto the voice of the Lord thy God.

3) Blessed shalt thou be in the city, and blessed shalt thou be in the field.

4) Blessed shall be the fruit of thy body, and the fruit of thy ground, and the fruit of thy cattle, the increase of thy kine, and the flocks of thy sheep.

5) Blessed shall be thy basket and thy store.

6) Blessed shalt thou be when thou comest in, and blessed shalt thou be when thou goest out.

7) The Lord shall cause thine enemies that rise up against thee to be smitten before thy face: they shall come out against thee one way, and flee before thee seven ways.

8)   The Lord shall command the blessing upon thee in thy storehouses, and in all that thou settest thine hand unto; and He shall bless thee in the land which the Lord thy God giveth thee.

9)   The Lord shall establish thee an holy people unto Himself, as He hath sworn unto thee, if thou shalt keep the commandments of the Lord thy God, and walk in His ways.

10)   And all people of the earth shall see that thou art called by the name of the Lord; and they shall be afraid of thee.

11)   And the Lord shall make thee plenteous in goods, in the fruit of thy body, and in the fruit of thy cattle, and in the fruit of thy ground, in the land which the Lord sware unto thy fathers to give thee.

12)   The Lord shall open unto thee His good treasure, the Heaven to give the rain unto thy land in his season, and to bless all the work of thine hand: and thou shalt lend unto many nations, and thou shalt not borrow.

13)   And the Lord shall make thee the head, and not the tail; and thou shalt be above only, and thou shalt not be beneath; if that thou hearken unto the commandments of the Lord thy God, which I command thee this day, to observe and to do them:

14)   And thou shalt not go aside from any of the words which I command thee this day, to the right hand, or to the left, to go after other gods to serve them.

CHAPTER 29

9)   Keep therefore the words of this covenant, and do them, that ye may prosper in all that ye do.

CHAPTER 30

5)   And the Lord thy God will bring thee into the land which thy fathers possessed, and thou shalt possess it; and He will do thee good, and multiply thee above thy fathers.

9)   And the Lord thy God will make thee plenteous in every work of thine hand, in the fruit of thy body, and in the fruit of thy cattle, and in the fruit of thy land, for good: for the Lord will again rejoice over thee for good, as He rejoiced over thy fathers:

10)   If thou shalt hearken unto the voice of the Lord thy God, to keep His commandments and His statutes which are written in this book of the law, and if thou turn unto the Lord thy God with all thine heart, and with all thy soul.

CHAPTER 32

6)   Do ye thus requite the Lord, O foolish people and unwise? is not He thy father that hath bought thee? hath He not made thee, and established thee?

9)   For the Lord's portion is His people; Jacob is the lot of His inheritance.

10)   He found him in a desert land, and in the waste howling wilderness; He led him about, He instructed him, He kept him as the apple of His eye.

11)   As an eagle stirreth up her nest, fluttereth over her young, spreadeth abroad her wings, taketh them, beareth them on her wings:

13)   He made him ride on the high places of the earth, that he might eat the increase of the fields; and He made him to suck honey out of the rock, and oil out of the flinty rock;

14) Butter of kine, and milk of sheep, with fat of lambs, and rams of the breed of Bashan, and goats, with the fat of kidneys of wheat; and thou didst drink the pure blood of the grape.

JOSHUA

CHAPTER 1

5) There shall not any man be able to stand before thee all the days of thy life: as I was with Moses, so I will be with thee: I will not fail thee, nor forsake thee.

6) Be strong and of a good courage: for unto this people shalt thou divide for an inheritance the land, which I sware unto their fathers to give them.

7) Only be thou strong and very courageous, that thou mayest observe to do according to all the law, which Moses My servant commanded thee: turn not from it to the right hand or to the left, that thou mayest prosper whithersoever thou goest.

8) This book of the law shall not depart out of thy mouth; but thou shalt meditate therein day and night, that thou mayest observe to do according to all that is written therein: for then thou shalt make thy way prosperous, and then thou shalt have good success.

9) Have not I commanded thee? Be strong and of a good courage; be not afraid, neither be thou dismayed: for the Lord thy God is with thee whithersoever thou goest.

CHAPTER 3

7) And the Lord said unto Joshua, This day will I begin to magnify thee in the sight of all Israel, that they may know that, as I was with Moses, so I will be with thee.

CHAPTER 10

25) And Joshua said unto them, Fear not, nor be dismayed, be strong and of good courage: for thus shall the Lord do to all your enemies against whom ye fight.

CHAPTER 23

5) And the Lord your God, He shall expel them from before you, and drive them from out of your sight; and ye shall possess their land, as the Lord your God hath promised unto you.

6) Be ye therefore very courageous to keep and to do all that is written in the book of the law of Moses, that ye turn not aside therefrom to the right hand or to the left;

7) That ye come not among these nations, these that remain among you; neither make mention of the name of their gods, nor cause to swear by them, neither serve them, nor bow yourselves unto them:

8) But cleave unto the Lord your God, as ye have done unto this day.

9) For the Lord hath driven out from before you great nations and strong: but as for you, no man hath been able to stand before you unto this day.

10) One man of you shall chase a thousand: for the Lord your God, He it is that fighteth for you, as He hath promised you.

1 SAMUEL

CHAPTER 2

8) He raiseth up the poor out of the dust, and lifteth up the beggar from the dunghill, to set them among princes, and to make them inherit the throne of glory: for the pillars of the earth are the Lord's, and He hath set the world upon them.

9) He will keep the feet of His saints, and the wicked shall be silent in darkness; for by strength shall no man prevail.

10) The adversaries of the Lord shall be broken to pieces; out of Heaven shall He thunder upon them: the Lord shall judge the ends of the earth; and He shall give strength unto His king, and exalt the horn of His anointed.

CHAPTER 12

16) Now therefore stand and see this great thing, which the Lord will do before your eyes.

CHAPTER 17

45) Then said David to the Philistine, Thou comest to me with a sword, and with a spear, and with a shield: but I come to thee in the name of the Lord of hosts, the God of the armies of Israel, whom thou hast defied.

46) This day will the Lord deliver thee into mine hand; and I will smite thee, and take thine head from thee; and I will give the carcases of the host of the Philistines this day unto the fowls of the air, and to the wild beasts of the earth; that all the earth may

know that there is a God in Israel.

47) And all this assembly shall know that the Lord saveth not with sword and spear: for the battle is the Lord's, and He will give you into our hands.

2 SAMUEL

CHAPTER 7

9) And I was with thee whithersoever thou wentest, and have cut off all thine enemies out of thy sight, and have made thee a great name, like unto the name of the great men that are in the earth.

10) Moreover I will appoint a place for My people Israel, and will plant them, that they may dwell in a place of their own, and move no more; neither shall the children of wickedness afflict them any more, as beforetime,

11) And as since the time that I commanded judges to be over My people Israel, and have caused thee to rest from all thine enemies. Also the Lord telleth thee that He will make thee an house.

12) And when thy days be fulfilled, and thou shalt sleep with thy fathers, I will set up thy Seed after thee, which shall proceed out of thy bowels, and I will establish His kingdom.

13) He shall build an house for My name, and I will stablish the throne of His kingdom for ever.

CHAPTER 22

17) He sent from above, He took me; He drew me out of many waters;

18) He delivered me from my strong enemy, and

from them that hated me: for they were too strong for me.

20) He brought me forth also into a large place: He delivered me, because He delighted in me.

29) For thou art my lamp, O Lord: and the Lord will lighten my darkness.

30) For by thee I have run through a troop: by my God have I leaped over a wall.

31) As for God, His way is perfect; the word of the Lord is tried: He is a buckler to all them that trust in Him.

32) For who is God, save the Lord? and who is a rock, save our God?

33) God is my strength and power: and He maketh my way perfect.

34) He maketh my feet like hinds' feet: and setteth me upon my high places.

35) He teacheth my hands to war; so that a bow of steel is broken by mine arms.

37) Thou hast enlarged my steps under me; so that my feet did not slip.

47) The Lord liveth; and blessed be my rock; and exalted be the God of the rock of my salvation.

48) It is God that avengeth me, and that bringeth down the people under me,

49) And that bringeth me forth from mine enemies: thou also hast lifted me up on high above them that rose up against me: thou hast delivered me from the violent man.

1 KINGS

CHAPTER 3

5)   In Gibeon the Lord appeared to Solomon in a dream by night: and God said, Ask what I shall give thee.

6)   And Solomon said, Thou hast shewed unto thy servant David my father great mercy, according as he walked before thee in truth, and in righteousness, and in uprightness of heart with thee; and thou hast kept for him this great kindness, that thou hast given him a son to sit on his throne, as it is this day.

7)   And now, O Lord my God, thou hast made thy servant king instead of David my father: and I am but a little child: I know not how to go out or come in.

8)   And thy servant is in the midst of thy people which thou hast chosen, a great people, that cannot be numbered nor counted for multitude.

9)   Give therefore thy servant an understanding heart to judge thy people, that I may discern between good and bad: for who is able to judge this thy so great a people?

10) And the speech pleased the Lord, that Solomon had asked this thing.

11) And God said unto him, Because thou hast asked this thing, and hast not asked for thyself long life; neither hast asked riches for thyself, nor hast asked the life of thine enemies; but hast asked for thyself understanding to discern judgment;

12) Behold, I have done according to thy words:

lo, I have given thee a wise and an understanding heart; so that there was none like thee before thee, neither after thee shall any arise like unto thee.

13) And I have also given thee that which thou hast not asked, both riches, and honour: so that there shall not be any among the kings like unto thee all thy days.

14) And if thou wilt walk in My ways, to keep My statutes and My commandments, as thy father David did walk, then I will lengthen thy days.

15) And Solomon awoke; and, behold, it was a dream. And he came to Jerusalem, and stood before the ark of the covenant of the Lord, and offered up burnt offerings, and offered peace offerings, and made a feast to all his servants.

CHAPTER 4

29) And God gave Solomon Wisdom and understanding exceeding much, and largeness of heart, even as the sand that is on the sea shore.

CHAPTER 8

56) Blessed be the Lord, that hath given rest unto His people Israel, according to all that He promised: there hath not failed one word of all His good promise, which He promised by the hand of Moses His servant.

CHAPTER 17

1) And Elijah the Tishbite, who was of the inhabitants of Gilead, said unto Ahab, As the Lord God of Israel liveth, before whom I stand, there shall

not be dew nor rain these years, but according to my word.

2) And the word of the Lord came unto him, saying,

3) Get thee hence, and turn thee eastward, and hide thyself by the brook Chcrith, that is before Jordan.

4) And it shall be, that thou shalt drink of the brook; and I have commanded the ravens to feed thee there.

5) So he went and did according unto the word of the Lord: for he went and dwelt by the brook Cherith, that is before Jordan.

6) And the ravens brought him bread and flesh in the morning, and bread and flesh in the evening; and he drank of the brook.

7) And it came to pass after a while, that the brook dried up, because there had been no rain in the land.

8) And the word of the Lord came unto him, saying,

9) Arise, get thee to Zarephath, which belongeth to Zidon, and dwell there: behold, I have commanded a widow woman there to sustain thee.

10) So he arose and went to Zarephath. And when he came to the gate of the city, behold, the widow woman was there gathering of sticks: and he called to her, and said, Fetch me, I pray thee, a little water in a vessel, that I may drink.

11) And as she was going to fetch it, he called to her, and said, Bring me, I pray thee, a morsel of bread in thine hand.

12) And she said, As the Lord thy God liveth, I

have not a cake, but an handful of meal in a barrel, and a little oil in a cruse: and, behold, I am gathering two sticks, that I may go in and dress it for me and my son, that we may eat it, and die.

13) And Elijah said unto her, Fear not; go and do as thou hast said: but make me thereof a little cake first, and bring it unto me, and after make for thee and for thy son.

14) For thus saith the Lord God of Israel, The barrel of meal shall not waste, neither shall the cruse of oil fail, until the day that the Lord sendeth rain upon the earth.

15) And she went and did according to the saying of Elijah: and she, and he, and her house, did eat many days.

16) And the barrel of meal wasted not, neither did the cruse of oil fail, according to the word of the Lord, which He spake by Elijah.

2 KINGS

CHAPTER 18

1) Now it came to pass in the third year of Hoshea son of Elah king of Israel, that Hezekiah the son of Ahaz king of Judah began to reign.

5) He trusted in the Lord God of Israel; so that after him was none like him among all the kings of Judah, nor any that were before him.

7) And the Lord was with him; and he prospered whithersoever he went forth: and he rebelled against the king of Assyria, and served him not.

1 CHRONICLES

CHAPTER 16

27) Glory and honour are in His presence; strength and gladness are in His place.

CHAPTER 22

11) Now, my son, the Lord be with thee; and prosper thou, and build the house of the Lord thy God, as He hath said of thee.

12) Only the Lord give thee Wisdom and understanding, and give thee charge concerning Israel, that thou mayest keep the law of the Lord thy God.

13) Then shalt thou prosper, if thou takest heed to fulfil the statutes and judgments which the Lord charged Moses with concerning Israel: be strong, and of good courage; dread not, nor be dismayed.

19) Now set your heart and your soul to seek the Lord your God; arise therefore, and build ye the sanctuary of the Lord God, to bring the ark of the covenant of the Lord, and the holy vessels of God, into the house that is to be built to the name of the Lord.

CHAPTER 28

20) And David said to Solomon his son, Be strong and of good courage, and do it: fear not, nor be dismayed: for the Lord God, even my God, will be with thee, he will not fail thee, nor forsake thee, until thou hast finished all the work for the service of the house of the Lord.

CHAPTER 29

11) Thine, O Lord, is the greatness, and the power, and the glory, and the victory, and the majesty: for all that is in the Heaven and in the earth is Thine; Thine is the kingdom, O Lord, and Thou art exalted as head above all.

12) Both riches and honour come of Thee, and Thou reignest over all; and in Thine hand is power and might; and in Thine hand it is to make great, and to give strength unto all.

2 CHRONICLES

CHAPTER 1

1) And Solomon the son of David was strengthened in his kingdom, and the Lord his God was with him, and magnified him exceedingly.

8) And Solomon said unto God, Thou hast shewed great mercy unto David my father, and hast made me to reign in his stead.

10) Give me now Wisdom and knowledge, that I may go out and come in before this people: for who can judge this Thy people, that is so great?

11) And God said to Solomon, Because this was in thine heart, and thou hast not asked riches, wealth, or honour, nor the life of thine enemies, neither yet hast asked long life; but hast asked Wisdom and knowledge for thyself, that thou mayest judge My people, over whom I have made thee king:

12) Wisdom and knowledge is granted unto thee; and I will give thee riches, and wealth, and honour, such as none of the kings have had that have been

before thee, neither shall there any after thee have the like.

CHAPTER 6

25) Then hear Thou from the Heavens, and forgive the sin of Thy people Israel, and bring them again unto the land which Thou gavest to them and to their fathers.

26) When the Heaven is shut up, and there is no rain, because they have sinned against Thee; yet if they pray toward this place, and confess Thy name, and turn from their sin, when Thou dost afflict them;

27) Then hear Thou from Heaven, and forgive the sin of Thy servants, and of Thy people Israel, when Thou hast taught them the good way, wherein they should walk; and send rain upon Thy land, which thou hast given unto Thy people for an inheritance.

28) If there be dearth in the land, if there be pestilence, if there be blasting, or mildew, locusts, or caterpillars; if their enemies besiege them in the cities of their land; whatsoever sore or whatsoever sickness there be:

29) Then what prayer or what supplication soever shall be made of any man, or of all Thy people Israel, when every one shall know his own sore and his own grief, and shall spread forth his hands in this house:

30) Then hear Thou from Heaven Thy dwelling place, and forgive, and render unto every man according unto all his ways, whose heart Thou knowest; (for Thou only knowest the hearts of the children of men:)

31) That they may fear Thee, to walk in Thy ways, so long as they live in the land which Thou gavest unto our fathers.

32) Moreover concerning the stranger, which is not of Thy people Israel, but is come from a far country for Thy great name's sake, and Thy mighty hand, and Thy stretched out arm; if they come and pray in this house;

33) Then hear Thou from the Heavens, even from Thy dwelling place, and do according to all that the stranger calleth to Thee for; that all people of the earth may know Thy name, and fear Thee, as doth Thy people Israel, and may know that this house which I have built is called by Thy name.

34) If Thy people go out to war against their enemies by the way that Thou shalt send them, and they pray unto Thee toward this city which thou hast chosen, and the house which I have built for Thy name;

35) Then hear Thou from the Heavens their prayer and their supplication, and maintain their cause.

36) If they sin against Thee, (for there is no man which sinneth not,) and Thou be angry with them, and deliver them over before their enemies, and they carry them away captives unto a land far off or near;

37) Yet if they bethink themselves in the land whither they are carried captive, and turn and pray unto Thee in the land of their captivity, saying, We have sinned, we have done amiss, and have dealt wickedly;

38) If they return to Thee with all their heart

and with all their soul in the land of their captivity, whither they have carried them captives, and pray toward their land, which Thou gavest unto their fathers, and toward the city which Thou hast chosen, and toward the house which I have built for Thy name:

39) Then hear Thou from the Heavens, even from Thy dwelling place, their prayer and their supplications, and maintain their cause, and forgive Thy people which have sinned against Thee.

40) Now, my God, let I beseech thee, Thine eyes be open, and let Thine ears be attent unto the prayer that is made in this place.

41) Now therefore arise, O Lord God, into Thy resting place, thou, and the ark of thy strength: let Thy priests, O Lord God, be clothed with salvation, and let Thy saints rejoice in goodness.

42) O Lord God, turn not away the face of Thine anointed: remember the mercies of David Thy servant.

CHAPTER 16
9) For the eyes of the Lord run to and fro throughout the whole earth, to shew Himself strong in the behalf of them whose heart is perfect toward Him.

CHAPTER 20
15) Be not afraid nor dismayed by reason of this great multitude; for the battle is not yours, but God's.

CHAPTER 26
5) And he sought God in the days of Zechariah,

who had understanding in the visions of God: and as long as he sought the Lord, God made him to prosper.

CHAPTER 30

9) For if ye turn again unto the Lord, your brethren and your children shall find compassion before them that lead them captive, so that they shall come again into this land: for the Lord your God is gracious and merciful, and will not turn away His face from you, if ye return unto Him.

CHAPTER 32

27) And Hezekiah had exceeding much riches and honour: and he made himself treasuries for silver, and for gold, and for precious stones, and for spices, and for shields, and for all manner of pleasant jewels;

28) Storehouses also for the increase of corn, and wine, and oil; and stalls for all manner of beasts, and cotes for flocks.

29) Moreover He provided him cities, and possessions of flocks and herds in abundance: for God had given him substance very much.

NEHEMIAH

CHAPTER 1

11) O Lord, I beseech Thee, let now Thine ear be attentive to the prayer of Thy servant, and to the prayer of Thy servants, who desire to fear Thy name: and prosper, I pray Thee, Thy servant this day, and

grant him mercy in the sight of this man. For I was the king's cupbearer.

CHAPTER 2

20) Then answered I them, and said unto them, The God of Heaven, He will prosper us; therefore we His servants will arise and build: but ye have no portion, nor right, nor memorial, in Jerusalem.

CHAPTER 8

10) Then he said unto them, Go your way, eat the fat, and drink the sweet, and send portions unto them for whom nothing is prepared: for this day is holy unto our Lord: neither be ye sorry; for the joy of the Lord is your strength.

CHAPTER 9

17) And refused to obey, neither were mindful of Thy wonders that Thou didst among them; but hardened their necks, and in their rebellion appointed a captain to return to their bondage: but Thou art a God ready to pardon, gracious and merciful, slow to anger, and of great kindness, and forsookest them not.

19) Yet Thou in Thy manifold mercies forsookest them not in the wilderness: the pillar of the cloud departed not from them by day, to lead them in the way; neither the pillar of fire by night, to shew them light, and the way wherein they should go.

20) Thou gavest also Thy good Spirit to instruct them, and withheldest not Thy manna from their mouth, and gavest them water for their thirst.

21) Yea, forty years didst Thou sustain them in the wilderness, so that they lacked nothing; their clothes waxed not old, and their feet swelled not.

22) Moreover Thou gavest them kingdoms and nations, and didst divide them into corners: so they possessed the land of Sihon, and the land of the king of Heshbon, and the land of Og king of Bashan.

23) Their children also multipliedst thou as the stars of Heaven, and broughtest them into the land, concerning which Thou hadst promised to their fathers, that they should go in to possess it.

24) So the children went in and possessed the land, and Thou subduedst before them the inhabitants of the land, the Canaanites, and gavest them into their hands, with their kings, and the people of the land, that they might do with them as they would.

25) And they took strong cities, and a fat land, and possessed houses full of all goods, wells digged, vineyards, and oliveyards, and fruit trees in abundance: so they did eat, and were filled, and became fat, and delighted themselves in Thy great goodness.

27) Therefore Thou deliveredst them into the hand of their enemies, who vexed them: and in the time of their trouble, when they cried unto Thee, Thou heardest them from Heaven; and according to Thy manifold mercies Thou gavest them saviours, who saved them out of the hand of their enemies.

31) Nevertheless for Thy great mercies' sake thou didst not utterly consume them, nor forsake them; for Thou art a gracious and merciful God.

32) Now therefore, our God, the great, the mighty, and the terrible God, who keepest covenant

and mercy, let not all the trouble seem little before thee, that hath come upon us, on our kings, on our princes, and on our priests, and on our prophets, and on our fathers, and on all Thy people, since the time of the kings of Assyria unto this day.

JOB

CHAPTER 1

1)   There was a man in the land of Uz, whose name was Job; and that man was perfect and upright, and one that feared God, and eschewed evil.

2)   And there were born unto him seven sons and three daughters.

3)   His substance also was seven thousand sheep, and three thousand camels, and five hundred yoke of oxen, and five hundred she asses, and a very great household; so that this man was the greatest of all the men of the east.

CHAPTER 4

4)   Thy words have upholden him that was falling, and thou hast strengthened the feeble knees.

CHAPTER 5

20)   In famine He shall redeem thee from death: and in war from the power of the sword.

21)   Thou shalt be hid from the scourge of the tongue: neither shalt thou be afraid of destruction when it cometh.

26)   Thou shalt come to thy grave in a full age, like as a shock of corn cometh in in his season.

CHAPTER 10

12) Thou hast granted me life and favour, and Thy visitation hath preserved my spirit.

CHAPTER 19

25) For I know that my redeemer liveth, and that He shall stand at the latter day upon the earth:

26) And though after my skin worms destroy this body, yet in my flesh shall I see God;

CHAPTER 22

21) Acquaint now thyself with Him, and be at peace: thereby good shall come unto thee.

22) Receive, I pray thee, the law from His mouth, and lay up His words in thine heart.

23) If thou return to the Almighty, thou shalt be built up, thou shalt put away iniquity far from thy tabernacles.

28) Thou shalt also decree a thing, and it shall be established unto thee: and the light shall shine upon thy ways.

CHAPTER 29

12) Because I delivered the poor that cried, and the fatherless, and him that had none to help.

13) The blessing of him that was ready to perish came upon me: and I caused the widow's heart to sing for joy.

CHAPTER 32

8) But there is a spirit in man: and the inspiration of the Almighty giveth them understanding.

CHAPTER 33

4)   The Spirit of God hath made me, and the breath of the Almighty hath given me life.

28)   He will deliver his soul from going into the pit, and his life shall see the light.

29)   Lo, all these things worketh God oftentimes with man,

30)   To bring back his soul from the pit, to be enlightened with the light of the living.

CHAPTER 36

7)   He withdraweth not His eyes from the righteous: but with kings are they on the throne; yea, He doth establish them for ever, and they are exalted.

11)   If they obey and serve Him, they shall spend their days in prosperity, and their years in pleasures.

15)   He delivereth the poor in His affliction, and openeth their ears in oppression.

CHAPTER 37

23)   Touching the Almighty, we cannot find Him out: He is excellent in power, and in judgment, and in plenty of justice: He will not afflict.

CHAPTER 42

10)   And the Lord turned the captivity of Job, when he prayed for his friends: also the Lord gave Job twice as much as he had before.

11)   Then came there unto him all his brethren, and all his sisters, and all they that had been of his acquaintance before, and did eat bread with him in his house: and they bemoaned him, and comforted

him over all the evil that the Lord had brought upon him: every man also gave him a piece of money, and every one an earring of gold.

12) So the Lord blessed the latter end of Job more than his beginning: for he had fourteen thousand sheep, and six thousand camels, and a thousand yoke of oxen, and a thousand she asses.

13) He had also seven sons and three daughters.

14) And he called the name of the first, Jemima; and the name of the second, Kezia; and the name of the third, Kerenhappuch.

15) And in all the land were no women found so fair as the daughters of Job: and their father gave them inheritance among their brethren.

16) After this lived Job an hundred and forty years, and saw his sons, and his sons' sons, even four generations.

17) So Job died, being old and full of days.

PSALMS

CHAPTER 1

1) Blessed is the man that walketh not in the counsel of the ungodly, nor standeth in the way of sinners, nor sitteth in the seat of the scornful.

2) But his delight is in the law of the Lord; and in His law doth he meditate day and night.

3) And he shall be like a tree planted by the rivers of water, that bringeth forth his fruit in his season; his leaf also shall not wither; and whatsoever he doeth shall prosper.

CHAPTER 2

8) Ask of Me, and I shall give thee the heathen for thine inheritance, and the uttermost parts of the earth for thy possession.

CHAPTER 3

2) Many there be which say of my soul, There is no help for him in God. Selah.

3) But Thou, O Lord, art a shield for me; my glory, and the lifter up of mine head.

4) I cried unto the Lord with my voice, and He heard me out of His holy hill. Selah.

5) I laid me down and slept; I awaked; for the Lord sustained me.

6) I will not be afraid of ten thousands of people, that have set themselves against me round about.

7) Arise, O Lord; save me, O my God: for Thou hast smitten all mine enemies upon the cheek bone; Thou hast broken the teeth of the ungodly.

8 Salvation belongeth unto the Lord: Thy blessing is upon Thy people. Selah.

CHAPTER 4

3) But know that the Lord hath set apart him that is godly for Himself: the Lord will hear when I call unto Him.

7) Thou hast put gladness in my heart, more than in the time that their corn and their wine increased.

8) I will both lay me down in peace, and sleep: for Thou, Lord, only makest me dwell in safety.

CHAPTER 5

11)   But let all those that put their trust in Thee rejoice: let them ever shout for joy, because Thou defendest them: let them also that love Thy name be joyful in Thee.

12)   For Thou, Lord, wilt bless the righteous; with favour wilt Thou compass him as with a shield.

CHAPTER 6

9)   The Lord hath heard my supplication; the Lord will receive my prayer.

CHAPTER 8

3)   When I consider Thy Heavens, the work of Thy fingers, the moon and the stars, which Thou hast ordained;

4)   What is man, that Thou art mindful of him? and the son of man, that Thou visitest him?

5)   For Thou hast made him a little lower than the angels, and hast crowned him with glory and honour.

6)   Thou madest him to have dominion over the works of Thy hands; Thou hast put all things under his feet:

7)   All sheep and oxen, yea, and the beasts of the field;

8)   The fowl of the air, and the fish of the sea, and whatsoever passeth through the paths of the seas.

CHAPTER 9

4)   For Thou hast maintained my right and my

cause; Thou sattest in the throne judging right.

CHAPTER 15

1) Lord, who shall abide in Thy tabernacle? who shall dwell in Thy holy hill?

2) He that walketh uprightly, and worketh righteousness, and speaketh the truth in his heart.

3) He that backbiteth not with his tongue, nor doeth evil to his neighbour, nor taketh up a reproach against his neighbour.

4) In whose eyes a vile person is contemned; but he honoureth them that fear the Lord. He that sweareth to his own hurt, and changeth not.

5) He that putteth not out his money to usury, nor taketh reward against the innocent. He that doeth these things shall never be moved.

CHAPTER 16

7) I will bless the Lord, who hath given me counsel: my reins also instruct me in the night seasons.

8) I have set the Lord always before me: because He is at my right hand, I shall not be moved.

9) Therefore my heart is glad, and my glory rejoiceth: my flesh also shall rest in hope.

10) For Thou wilt not leave my soul in hell; neither wilt Thou suffer thine Holy One to see corruption.

11) Thou wilt shew me the path of life: in Thy presence is fulness of joy; at Thy right hand there are pleasures for evermore.

CHAPTER 17

15) As for me, I will behold Thy face in righteousness: I shall be satisfied, when I awake, with Thy likeness.

CHAPTER 18

2) The Lord is my rock, and my fortress, and my deliverer; my God, my strength, in Whom I will trust; my buckler, and the horn of my salvation, and my high tower.

6) In my distress I called upon the Lord, and cried unto my God: He heard my voice out of His temple, and my cry came before Him, even into His ears.

16) He sent from above, He took me, He drew me out of many waters.

17) He delivered me from my strong enemy, and from them which hated me: for they were too strong for me.

18) They prevented me in the day of my calamity: but the Lord was my stay.

19) He brought me forth also into a large place; He delivered me, because He delighted in me.

25) With the merciful Thou wilt shew Thyself merciful; with an upright man Thou wilt shew Thyself upright;

26) With the pure Thou wilt shew Thyself pure; and with the froward Thou wilt shew Thyself froward.

28) For Thou wilt light my candle: the Lord my God will enlighten my darkness.

29) For by Thee I have run through a troop; and by my God have I leaped over a wall.

32)   It is God that girdeth me with strength, and maketh my way perfect.

33)   He maketh my feet like hinds' feet, and setteth me upon my high places.

34)   He teacheth my hands to war, so that a bow of steel is broken by mine arms.

35)   Thou hast also given me the shield of Thy salvation: and Thy right hand hath holden me up, and Thy gentleness hath made me great.

36)   Thou hast enlarged my steps under me, that my feet did not slip.

39)   For Thou hast girded me with strength unto the battle: Thou hast subdued under me those that rose up against me.

43)   Thou hast delivered me from the strivings of the people; and Thou hast made me the head of the heathen: a people whom I have not known shall serve me.

44)   As soon as they hear of me, they shall obey me: the strangers shall submit themselves unto me.

45)   The strangers shall fade away, and be afraid out of their close places.

46)   The Lord liveth; and blessed be my rock; and let the God of my salvation be exalted.

47)   It is God that avengeth me, and subdueth the people under me.

48)   He delivereth me from mine enemies: yea, Thou liftest me up above those that rise up against me: Thou hast delivered me from the violent man.

CHAPTER 19

7)   The law of the Lord is perfect, converting the soul: the testimony of the Lord is sure, making

wise the simple.

8)   The statutes of the Lord are right, rejoicing the heart: the commandment of the Lord is pure, enlightening the eyes.

9)   The fear of the Lord is clean, enduring for ever: the judgments of the Lord are true and righteous altogether.

10) More to be desired are they than gold, yea, than much fine gold: sweeter also than honey and the honeycomb.

11) Moreover by them is Thy servant warned: and in keeping of them there is great reward.

CHAPTER 20

6)   Now know I that the Lord saveth His anointed; He will hear Him from His holy Heaven with the saving strength of His right hand.

7)   Some trust in chariots, and some in horses: but we will remember the name of the Lord our God.

8)   They are brought down and fallen: but we are risen, and stand upright.

CHAPTER 21

1)   The king shall joy in Thy strength, O Lord; and in Thy salvation how greatly shall he rejoice!

2)   Thou hast given him his heart's desire, and hast not withholden the request of his lips. Selah.

3)   For Thou preventest him with the blessings of goodness: Thou settest a crown of pure gold on his head.

4)   He asked life of Thee, and Thou gavest it him, even length of days for ever and ever.

5)   His glory is great in Thy salvation: honour

and majesty hast Thou laid upon him.

6) For Thou hast made him most blessed for ever: Thou hast made him exceeding glad with Thy countenance.

7) For the king trusteth in the Lord, and through the mercy of the most High he shall not be moved.

CHAPTER 22

26) The meek shall eat and be satisfied: they shall praise the Lord that seek Him: your heart shall live for ever.

CHAPTER 23

1) The Lord is my shepherd; I shall not want.

2) He maketh me to lie down in green pastures: He leadeth me beside the still waters.

3) He restoreth my soul: He leadeth me in the paths of righteousness for His name's sake.

4) Yea, though I walk through the valley of the shadow of death, I will fear no evil: for Thou art with me; Thy rod and Thy staff they comfort me.

5) Thou preparest a table before me in the presence of mine enemies: Thou anointest my head with oil; my cup runneth over.

6) Surely goodness and mercy shall follow me all the days of my life: and I will dwell in the house of the Lord for ever.

CHAPTER 24

4) He that hath clean hands, and a pure heart; who hath not lifted up his soul unto vanity, nor sworn deceitfully.

5) He shall receive the blessing from the Lord, and righteousness from the God of his salvation.

CHAPTER 25

8) Good and upright is the Lord: therefore will He teach sinners in the way.

9) The meek will He guide in judgment: and the meek will He teach His way.

12) What man is he that feareth the Lord? him shall He teach in the way that he shall choose.

13) His soul shall dwell at ease; and his Seed shall inherit the earth.

14) The secret of the Lord is with them that fear him; and He will shew them His covenant.

CHAPTER 26

1) Judge me, O Lord; for I have walked in mine integrity: I have trusted also in the Lord; therefore I shall not slide.

CHAPTER 27

1) The Lord is my light and my salvation; whom shall I fear? the Lord is the strength of my life; of whom shall I be afraid?

2) When the wicked, even mine enemies and my foes, came upon me to eat up my flesh, they stumbled and fell.

3) Though an host should encamp against me, my heart shall not fear: though war should rise against me, in this will I be confident.

4) One thing have I desired of the Lord, that will I seek after; that I may dwell in the house of the

Lord all the days of my life, to behold the beauty of the Lord, and to inquire in His temple.

5) For in the time of trouble He shall hide me in His pavilion: in the secret of His tabernacle shall He hide me; He shall set me up upon a rock.

6) And now shall mine head be lifted up above mine enemies round about me: therefore will I offer in His tabernacle sacrifices of joy; I will sing, yea, I will sing praises unto the Lord.

13) I had fainted, unless I had believed to see the goodness of the Lord in the land of the living.

14) Wait on the Lord: be of good courage, and He shall strengthen thine heart: wait, I say, on the Lord.

CHAPTER 28

5) Because they regard not the works of the Lord, nor the operation of His hands, He shall destroy them, and not build them up.

6) Blessed be the Lord, because He hath heard the voice of my supplications.

7) The Lord is my strength and my shield; my heart trusted in Him, and I am helped: therefore my heart greatly rejoiceth; and with my song will I praise Him.

8) The Lord is their strength, and He is the saving strength of His anointed.

CHAPTER 29

11) The Lord will give strength unto His people; the Lord will bless His people with peace.

CHAPTER 30

1)   I will extol thee, O Lord; for Thou hast lifted me up, and hast not made my foes to rejoice over me.

2)   O Lord my God, I cried unto Thee, and Thou hast healed me.

3)   O Lord, Thou hast brought up my soul from the grave: Thou hast kept me alive, that I should not go down to the pit.

5)   For His anger endureth but a moment; in His favour is life: weeping may endure for a night, but joy cometh in the morning.

6)   And in my prosperity I said, I shall never be moved.

CHAPTER 31

19)   Oh how great is Thy goodness, which Thou hast laid up for them that fear Thee; which Thou hast wrought for them that trust in Thee before the sons of men!

20)   Thou shalt hide them in the secret of Thy presence from the pride of man: thou shalt keep them secretly in a pavilion from the strife of tongues.

21)   Blessed be the Lord: for He hath shewed me His marvellous kindness in a strong city.

23)   O love the Lord, all ye His saints: for the Lord preserveth the faithful, and plentifully rewardeth the proud doer.

24)   Be of good courage, and He shall strengthen your heart, all ye that hope in the Lord.

CHAPTER 32

1)   Blessed is he whose transgression is forgiven, whose sin is covered.

2)   Blessed is the man unto whom the Lord imputeth not iniquity, and in whose spirit there is no guile.

7)   Thou art my hiding place; Thou shalt preserve me from trouble; Thou shalt compass me about with songs of deliverance. Selah.

8)   I will instruct Thee and teach Thee in the way which thou shalt go. I will guide thee with Mine eye.

CHAPTER 33

8)   Let all the earth fear the Lord: let all the inhabitants of the world stand in awe of Him.

9)   For He spake, and it was done; He commanded, and it stood fast.

10)   The Lord bringeth the counsel of the heathen to nought: He maketh the devices of the people of none effect.

12)   Blessed is the nation whose God is the Lord; and the people whom He hath chosen for His own inheritance.

18)   Behold, the eye of the Lord is upon them that fear Him, upon them that hope in His mercy;

19)   To deliver their soul from death, and to keep them alive in famine.

20)   Our soul waiteth for the Lord: He is our help and our shield.

CHAPTER 34

4)   I sought the Lord, and He heard me, and delivered me from all my fears.

6)   This poor man cried, and the Lord heard him, and saved him out of all his troubles.

7) The angel of the Lord encampeth round about them that fear Him, and delivereth them.

8) O taste and see that the Lord is good: blessed is the man that trusteth in Him.

9) O fear the Lord, ye His saints: for there is no want to them that fear Him.

10) The young lions do lack, and suffer hunger: but they that seek the Lord shall not want any good thing.

15) The eyes of the Lord are upon the righteous, and His ears are open unto their cry.

17) The righteous cry, and the Lord heareth, and delivereth them out of all their troubles.

18) The Lord is nigh unto them that are of a broken heart; and saveth such as be of a contrite spirit.

20) He keepeth all His bones: not one of them is broken.

22) The Lord redeemeth the soul of His servants: and none of them that trust in Him shall be desolate.

CHAPTER 35

9) And my soul shall be joyful in the Lord: it shall rejoice in His salvation.

10) All my bones shall say, Lord, who is like unto thee, which deliverest the poor from him that is too strong for him, yea, the poor and the needy from him that spoileth him?

27) Let them shout for joy, and be glad, that favour my righteous cause: yea, let them say continually, Let the Lord be magnified, which hath pleasure in the prosperity of His servant.

CHAPTER 36

5)   Thy mercy, O Lord, is in the Heavens; and Thy faithfulness reacheth unto the clouds.

6)   Thy righteousness is like the great mountains; Thy judgments are a great deep: O Lord, Thou preservest man and beast.

7)   How excellent is Thy lovingkindness, O God! therefore the children of men put their trust under the shadow of Thy wings.

8)   They shall be abundantly satisfied with the fatness of Thy house; and thou shalt make them drink of the river of Thy pleasures.

9)   For with thee is the fountain of life: in Thy light shall we see light.

CHAPTER 37

3)   Trust in the Lord, and do good; so shalt thou dwell in the land, and verily thou shalt be fed.

4)   Delight thyself also in the Lord; and He shall give thee the desires of thine heart.

5)   Commit thy way unto the Lord; trust also in Him; and He shall bring it to pass.

6)   And He shall bring forth thy righteousness as the light, and thy judgment as the noonday.

9)   For evildoers shall be cut off: but those that wait upon the Lord, they shall inherit the earth.

11)   But the meek shall inherit the earth; and shall delight themselves in the abundance of peace.

16)   A little that a righteous man hath is better than the riches of many wicked.

17)   For the arms of the wicked shall be broken: but the Lord upholdeth the righteous.

18)   The Lord knoweth the days of the upright:

and their inheritance shall be for ever.

19)   They shall not be ashamed in the evil time: and in the days of famine they shall be satisfied.

23)   The steps of a good man are ordered by the Lord: and he delighteth in His way.

24)   Though he fall, he shall not be utterly cast down: for the Lord upholdeth him with His hand.

25)   I have been young, and now am old; yet have I not seen the righteous forsaken, nor his Seed begging bread.

26)   He is ever merciful, and lendeth; and his Seed is blessed.

27)   Depart from evil, and do good; and dwell for evermore.

28)   For the Lord loveth judgment, and forsaketh not His saints; they are preserved for ever: but the Seed of the wicked shall be cut off.

29)   The righteous shall inherit the land, and dwell therein for ever.

31)   The law of his God is in his heart; none of his steps shall slide.

34)   Wait on the Lord, and keep His way, and He shall exalt thee to inherit the land: when the wicked are cut off, thou shalt see it.

37)   Mark the perfect man, and behold the upright: for the end of that man is peace.

39)   But the salvation of the righteous is of the Lord: He is their strength in the time of trouble.

40)   And the Lord shall help them, and deliver them: He shall deliver them from the wicked, and save them, because they trust in Him.

CHAPTER 40

1)   I waited patiently for the Lord; and He

inclined unto me, and heard my cry.

2)   He brought me up also out of an horrible pit, out of the miry clay, and set my feet upon a rock, and established my goings.

3)   And He hath put a new song in my mouth, even praise unto our God: many shall see it, and fear, and shall trust in the Lord.

4)   Blessed is that man that maketh the Lord his trust, and respecteth not the proud, nor such as turn aside to lies.

5)   Many, O Lord my God, are Thy wonderful works which thou hast done, and Thy thoughts which are to us-ward: they cannot be reckoned up in order unto Thee: if I would declare and speak of them, they are more than can be numbered.

17) But I am poor and needy; yet thc Lord thinketh upon me: Thou art my help and my deliverer; make no tarrying, O my God.

CHAPTER 41

1)   Blessed is he that considereth the poor: the Lord will deliver him in time of trouble.

2)   The Lord will preserve him, and keep him alive; and he shall be blessed upon the earth: and Thou wilt not deliver him unto the will of his enemies.

3)   The Lord will strengthen him upon the bed of languishing: Thou wilt make all his bed in his sickness.

11) By this I know that Thou favourest me, because mine enemy doth not triumph over me.

12) And as for me, Thou upholdest me in mine integrity, and settest me before Thy face for ever.

CHAPTER 42

8) Yet the Lord will command His lovingkindness in the daytime, and in the night His song shall be with me, and my prayer unto the God of my life.

11) Why art thou cast down, O my soul? and why art thou disquieted within me? hope thou in God: for I shall yet praise him, who is the health of my countenance, and my God.

CHAPTER 43

4) Then will I go unto the altar of God, unto God my exceeding joy: yea, upon the harp will I praise thee, O God my God.

5) Why art thou cast down, O my soul? and why art thou disquieted within me? hope in God: for I shall yet praise Him, who is the health of my countenance, and my God.

CHAPTER 44

5) Through Thee will we push down our enemies: through Thy name will we tread them under that rise up against us.

7) But Thou hast saved us from our enemies, and hast put them to shame that hated us.

CHAPTER 45

7) Thou lovest righteousness, and hatest wickedness: therefore God, thy God, hath anointed thee with the oil of gladness above thy fellows.

CHAPTER 46

1) God is our refuge and strength, a very

present help in trouble.

2)   Therefore will not we fear, though the earth be removed, and though the mountains be carried into the midst of the sea;

3)   Though the waters thereof roar and be troubled, though the mountains shake with the swelling thereof. Selah.

4)   There is a river, the streams whereof shall make glad the city of God, the holy place of the tabernacles of the most High.

5)   God is in the midst of her; she shall not be moved: God shall help her, and that right early.

7)   The Lord of hosts is with us; the God of Jacob is our refuge. Selah.

CHAPTER 50

15)   And call upon Me in the day of trouble: I will deliver thee, and thou shalt glorify Me.

CHAPTER 54

4)   Behold, God is mine helper: the Lord is with them that uphold my soul.

5)   He shall reward evil unto mine enemies: cut them off in thy truth.

6)   I will freely sacrifice unto Thee: I will praise Thy name, O Lord; for it is good.

7)   For He hath delivered me out of all trouble: and mine eye hath seen His desire upon mine enemies.

CHAPTER 55

16)   As for me, I will call upon God; and the Lord shall save me.

17) Evening, and morning, and at noon, will I pray, and cry aloud: and He shall hear my voice.

18) He hath delivered my soul in peace from the battle that was against me: for there were many with me.

22) Cast thy burden upon the Lord, and He shall sustain thee: He shall never suffer the righteous to be moved.

CHAPTER 56

3) What time I am afraid, I will trust in Thee.

4) In God I will praise His word, in God I have put my trust; I will not fear what flesh can do unto me.

9) When I cry unto thee, then shall mine enemies turn back: this I know; for God is for me.

10) In God will I praise His word: in the Lord will I praise His word.

11) In God have I put my trust: I will not be afraid what man can do unto me.

13) For Thou hast delivered my soul from death: wilt not Thou deliver my feet from falling, that I may walk before God in the light of the living?

CHAPTER 57

2) I will cry unto God most high; unto God that performeth all things for me.

3) He shall send from Heaven, and save me from the reproach of him that would swallow me up. Selah. God shall send forth His mercy and His truth.

CHAPTER 58

10) The righteous shall rejoice when he seeth

the vengeance: he shall wash his feet in the blood of the wicked.

CHAPTER 59

9) Because of His strength will I wait upon thee: for God is my defence.

10) The God of my mercy shall prevent me: God shall let me see my desire upon mine enemies.

16) But I will sing of Thy power; yea, I will sing aloud of Thy mercy in the morning: for Thou hast been my defence and refuge in the day of my trouble.

17) Unto Thee, O my strength, will I sing: for God is my defence, and the God of my mercy.

CHAPTER 60

12) Through God we shall do valiantly: for He it is that shall tread down our enemies.

CHAPTER 61

3) For Thou hast been a shelter for me, and a strong tower from the enemy.

4) I will abide in Thy tabernacle for ever: I will trust in the covert of thy wings. Selah.

5) For Thou, O God, hast heard my vows: Thou hast given me the heritage of those that fear Thy name.

CHAPTER 62

2) He only is my rock and my salvation; He is my defence; I shall not be greatly moved.

7) In God is my salvation and my glory: the rock of my strength, and my refuge, is in God.

8) Trust in Him at all times; ye people, pour out your heart before Him: God is a refuge for us. Selah.

12) Also unto Thee, O Lord, belongeth mercy: for Thou renderest to every man according to his work.

CHAPTER 63

3) Because Thy lovingkindness is better than life, my lips shall praise Thee.

4) Thus will I bless Thee while I live: I will lift up my hands in Thy name.

5) My soul shall be satisfied as with marrow and fatness; and my mouth shall praise Thee with joyful lips:

6) When I remember Thee upon my bed, and meditate on Thee in the night watches.

7) Because Thou hast been my help, therefore in the shadow of Thy wings will I rejoice:

8) My soul followeth hard after Thee: Thy right hand upholdeth me.

CHAPTER 64

10) The righteous shall be glad in the Lord, and shall trust in Him; and all the upright in heart shall glory.

CHAPTER 65

4) Blessed is the man whom Thou choosest, and causest to approach unto Thee, that he may dwell in Thy courts: we shall be satisfied with the goodness of Thy house, even of Thy holy temple.

9) Thou visitest the earth, and waterest it:

Thou greatly enrichest it with the river of God, which is full of water: Thou preparest them corn, when Thou hast so provided for it.

10) Thou waterest the ridges thereof abundantly: Thou settlest the furrows thereof: Thou makest it soft with showers: Thou blessest the springing thereof.

11) Thou crownest the year with thy goodness; and Thy paths drop fatness.

12) They drop upon the pastures of the wilderness: and the little hills rejoice on every side.

13) The pastures are clothed with flocks; the valleys also are covered over with corn; they shout for joy, they also sing.

CHAPTER 66

8)   O bless our God, ye people, and make the voice of His praise to be heard:

9)   Which holdeth our soul in life, and suffereth not our feet to be moved.

12)   Thou hast caused men to ride over our heads; we went through fire and through water: but Thou broughtest us out into a wealthy place.

16)   Come and hear, all ye that fear God, and I will declare what He hath done for my soul.

18)   If I regard iniquity in my heart, the Lord will not hear me:

19)   But verily God hath heard me; He hath attended to the voice of my prayer.

20)   Blessed be God, which hath not turned away my prayer, nor His mercy from me.

CHAPTER 67

1)   God be merciful unto us, and bless us; and cause His face to shine upon us; Selah.

2)   That Thy way may be known upon earth, Thy saving health among all nations.

5)   Let the people praise Thee, O God; let all the people praise Thee.

6)   Then shall the earth yield her increase; and God, even our own God, shall bless us.

7)   God shall bless us; and all the ends of the earth shall fear Him.

CHAPTER 68

3)   But let the righteous be glad; let them rejoice before God: yea, let them exceedingly rejoice.

4)   Sing unto God, sing praises to His name: extol Him that rideth upon the Heavens by His name JAH, and rejoice before Him.

5)   A father of the fatherless, and a judge of the widows, is God in His holy habitation.

6)   God setteth the solitary in families: He bringeth out those which are bound with chains: but the rebellious dwell in a dry land.

9)   Thou, O God, didst send a plentiful rain, whereby Thou didst confirm Thine inheritance, when it was weary.

10)   Thy congregation hath dwelt therein: Thou, O God, hast prepared of Thy goodness for the poor.

11)   The Lord gave the word: great was the company of those that published it.

19)   Blessed be the Lord, Who daily loadeth us with benefits, even the God of our salvation. Selah.

35)   O God, Thou art terrible out of Thy holy

places: the God of Israel is He that giveth strength and power unto His people. Blessed be God.

CHAPTER 69

32) The humble shall see this, and be glad: and your heart shall live that seek God.

33) For the Lord heareth the poor, and despiseth not His prisoners.

34) Let the Heaven and earth praise Him, the seas, and every thing that moveth therein.

35) For God will save Zion, and will build the cities of Judah: that they may dwell there, and have it in possession.

36) The Seed also of His servants shall inherit it: and they that love His name shall dwell therein.

CHAPTER 71

3) Be Thou my strong habitation, whereunto I may continually resort: Thou hast given commandment to save me; for thou art my rock and my fortress.

5) For Thou art my hope, O Lord God: Thou art my trust from my youth.

6) By Thee have I been holden up from the womb: Thou art He that took me out of my mother's bowels: my praise shall be continually of Thee.

7) I am as a wonder unto many; but Thou art my strong refuge.

16) I will go in the strength of the Lord God: I will make mention of Thy righteousness, even of thine only.

19) Thy righteousness also, O God, is very high, Who hast done great things: O God, who is like unto

Thee!

20)   Thou, which hast shewed me great and sore troubles, shalt quicken me again, and shalt bring me up again from the depths of the earth.

21)   Thou shalt increase my greatness, and comfort me on every side.

23)   My lips shall greatly rejoice when I sing unto Thee; and my soul, which Thou hast redeemed.

CHAPTER 72

4)   He shall judge the poor of the people, He shall save the children of the needy, and shall break in pieces the oppressor.

7)   In His days shall the righteous flourish; and abundance of peace so long as the moon endureth.

12)   For He shall deliver the needy when he crieth; the poor also, and him that hath no helper.

13)   He shall spare the poor and needy, and shall save the souls of the needy.

14)   He shall redeem their soul from deceit and violence: and precious shall their blood be in His sight.

17)   His name shall endure for ever: His name shall be continued as long as the sun: and men shall be blessed in Him: all nations shall call Him blessed.

18)   Blessed be the Lord God, the God of Israel, Who only doeth wondrous things.

CHAPTER 73

1)   Truly God is good to Israel, even to such as are of a clean heart.

23)   Nevertheless I am continually with thee: Thou hast holden me by my right hand.

24) Thou shalt guide me with Thy counsel, and afterward receive me to glory.

25) Whom have I in Heaven but Thee? and there is none upon earth that I desire beside Thee.

26) My flesh and my heart faileth: but God is the strength of my heart, and my portion for ever.

28) But it is good for me to draw near to God: I have put my trust in the Lord God, that I may declare all Thy works.

CHAPTER 77

1) I cried unto God with my voice, even unto God with my voice; and He gave ear unto me.

14) Thou art the God that doest wonders: Thou hast declared thy strength among the people.

15) Thou hast with thine arm redeemed Thy people, the sons of Jacob and Joseph. Selah.

CHAPTER 84

4) Blessed are they that dwell in Thy house: they will be still praising Thee. Selah.

5) Blessed is the man whose strength is in Thee; in whose heart are the ways of them.

6) Who passing through the valley of Baca make it a well; the rain also filleth the pools.

7) They go from strength to strength, every one of them in Zion appeareth before God.

11) For the Lord God is a sun and shield: the Lord will give grace and glory: no good thing will He withhold from them that walk uprightly.

12) O Lord of hosts, blessed is the man that trusteth in Thee.

CHAPTER 85

1) Lord, Thou hast been favourable unto Thy land: Thou hast brought back the captivity of Jacob.

2) Thou hast forgiven the iniquity of Thy people, Thou hast covered all their sin. Selah.

3) Thou hast taken away all Thy wrath: Thou hast turned Thyself from the fierceness of Thine anger.

12) Yea, the Lord shall give that which is good; and our land shall yield her increase.

CHAPTER 86

5) For Thou, Lord, art good, and ready to forgive; and plenteous in mercy unto all them that call upon Thee.

7) In the day of my trouble I will call upon Thee: for Thou wilt answer me.

10) For Thou art great, and doest wondrous things: Thou art God alone.

13) For great is Thy mercy toward me: and Thou hast delivered my soul from the lowest hell.

15) But Thou, O Lord, art a God full of compassion, and gracious, longsuffering, and plenteous in mercy and truth.

CHAPTER 89

8) O Lord God of hosts, Who is a strong Lord like unto Thee? or to Thy faithfulness round about Thee?

13) Thou hast a mighty arm: strong is Thy hand, and high is Thy right hand.

14) Justice and judgment are the habitation of Thy throne: mercy and truth shall go before Thy

face.

15) Blessed is the people that know the joyful sound: they shall walk, O Lord, in the light of Thy countenance.

16) In Thy name shall they rejoice all the day: and in Thy righteousness shall they be exalted.

17) For Thou art the glory of their strength: and in Thy favour our horn shall be exalted.

18) For the Lord is our defence; and the Holy One of Israel is our king.

33) Nevertheless my lovingkindness will I not utterly take from Him, nor suffer my faithfulness to fail.

34) My covenant will I not break, nor alter the thing that is gone out of my lips.

CHAPTER 91

1) He that dwelleth in the secret place of the most High shall abide under the shadow of the Almighty.

2) I will say of the Lord, He is my refuge and my fortress: my God; in Him will I trust.

3) Surely He shall deliver thee from the snare of the fowler, and from the noisome pestilence.

4) He shall cover thee with His feathers, and under His wings shalt thou trust: His truth shall be thy shield and buckler.

5) Thou shalt not be afraid for the terror by night; nor for the arrow that flieth by day;

6) Nor for the pestilence that walketh in darkness; nor for the destruction that wasteth at noonday.

7) A thousand shall fall at thy side, and ten

thousand at thy right hand; but it shall not come nigh thee.

8) Only with thine eyes shalt thou behold and see the reward of the wicked.

9) Because thou hast made the Lord, which is my refuge, even the most High, thy habitation;

10) There shall no evil befall thee, neither shall any plague come nigh thy dwelling.

11) For He shall give His angels charge over thee, to keep thee in all thy ways.

12) They shall bear thee up in their hands, lest thou dash thy foot against a stone.

13) Thou shalt tread upon the lion and adder: the young lion and the dragon shalt thou trample under feet.

14) Because He hath set His love upon me, therefore will I deliver him: I will set him on high, because He hath known My name.

15) He shall call upon Me, and I will answer him: I will be with him in trouble; I will deliver him, and honour him.

16) With long life will I satisfy him, and shew him My salvation.

CHAPTER 92

4) For thou, Lord, hast made me glad through Thy work: I will triumph in the works of Thy hands.

5) O Lord, how great are Thy works! and Thy thoughts are very deep.

10) But my horn shalt thou exalt like the horn of an unicorn: I shall be anointed with fresh oil.

11) Mine eye also shall see my desire on mine

enemies, and mine ears shall hear my desire of the wicked that rise up against me.

12) The righteous shall flourish like the palm tree: he shall grow like a cedar in Lebanon.

13) Those that be planted in the house of the Lord shall flourish in the courts of our God.

14) They shall still bring forth fruit in old age; they shall be fat and flourishing;

CHAPTER 94

9) He that planted the ear, shall He not hear? He that formed the eye, shall He not see?

10) He that chastiseth the heathen, shall not He correct? He that teacheth man knowledge, shall not He know?

12) Blessed is the man whom Thou chastenest, O Lord, and teachest him out of Thy law;

13) That Thou mayest give him rest from the days of adversity, until the pit be digged for the wicked.

14) For the Lord will not cast off His people, neither will He forsake His inheritance.

15) But judgment shall return unto righteousness: and all the upright in heart shall follow it.

17) Unless the Lord had been my help, my soul had almost dwelt in silence.

22) But the Lord is my defence; and my God is the rock of my refuge.

CHAPTER 97

10) Ye that love the Lord, hate evil: He preserveth the souls of His saints; He delivereth them out of the hand of the wicked.

11) Light is sown for the righteous, and gladness for the upright in heart.

CHAPTER 102

17) He will regard the prayer of the destitute, and not despise their prayer.

18) This shall be written for the generation to come: and the people which shall be created shall praise the Lord.

19) For He hath looked down from the height of His sanctuary; from Heaven did the Lord behold the earth;

20) To hear the groaning of the prisoner; to loose those that are appointed to death;

24) I said, O my God, take me not away in the midst of my days: Thy years are throughout all generations.

26) They shall perish, but thou shalt endure: yea, all of them shall wax old like a garment; as a vesture shalt Thou change them, and they shall be changed:

28) The children of Thy servants shall continue, and their Seed shall be established before Thee.

CHAPTER 103

1) Bless the Lord, O my soul: and all that is within me, bless His holy name.

2) Bless the Lord, O my soul, and forget not all His benefits:

3) Who forgiveth all thine iniquities; Who healeth all thy diseases;

4) Who redeemeth thy life from destruction;

who crowneth thee with lovingkindness and tender mercies;

5)   Who satisfieth thy mouth with good things; so that thy youth is renewed like the eagle's.

6)   The Lord executeth righteousness and judgment for all that are oppressed.

7)   He made known His ways unto Moses, His acts unto the children of Israel.

8)   The Lord is merciful and gracious, slow to anger, and plenteous in mercy.

9)   He will not always chide: neither will He keep His anger for ever.

10) He hath not dealt with us after our sins; nor rewarded us according to our iniquities.

11) For as the Heaven is high above the earth, so great is His mercy toward them that fear Him.

12) As far as the east is from the west, so far hath He removed our transgressions from us.

13) Like as a father pitieth his children, so the Lord pitieth them that fear Him.

14) For He knoweth our frame; He remembereth that we are dust.

15) As for man, his days are as grass: as a flower of the field, so he flourisheth.

16) For the wind passeth over it, and it is gone; and the place thereof shall know it no more.

17) But the mercy of the Lord is from everlasting to everlasting upon them that fear Him, and His righteousness unto children's children;

18) To such as keep His covenant, and to those that remember His commandments to do them.

19) The Lord hath prepared His throne in the Heavens; and His kingdom ruleth over all.

20) Bless the Lord, ye His angels, that excel in strength, that do His commandments, hearkening unto the voice of His word.

21) Bless ye the Lord, all ye His hosts; ye ministers of His, that do His pleasure.

22) Bless the Lord, all His works in all places of His dominion: bless the Lord, O my soul.

CHAPTER 104

5) Who laid the foundations of the earth, that it should not be removed for ever.

13) He watereth the hills from His chambers: the earth is satisfied with the fruit of Thy works.

14) He causeth the grass to grow for the cattle, and herb for the service of man: that He may bring forth food out of the earth;

15) And wine that maketh glad the heart of man, and oil to make His face to shine, and bread which strengtheneth man's heart.

24) O Lord, how manifold are Thy works! in Wisdom hast Thou made them all: the earth is full of Thy riches.

27) These wait all upon Thee; that Thou mayest give them their meat in due season.

28) That Thou givest them they gather: Thou openest Thine hand, they are filled with good.

CHAPTER 105

14) He suffered no man to do them wrong: yea, He reproved kings for their sakes;

15) Saying, Touch not Mine anointed, and do My prophets no harm.

24) And He increased His people greatly; and

made them stronger than their enemies.

37) He brought them forth also with silver and gold: and there was not one feeble person among their tribes.

38) Egypt was glad when they departed: for the fear of them fell upon them.

39) He spread a cloud for a covering; and fire to give light in the night.

40) The people asked, and He brought quails, and satisfied them with the bread of Heaven.

41) He opened the rock, and the waters gushed out; they ran in the dry places like a river.

42) For He remembered His holy promise, and Abraham His servant.

43) And He brought forth His people with joy, and His chosen with gladness:

44) And gave them the lands of the heathen: and they inherited the labour of the people;

CHAPTER 106

3) Blessed are they that keep judgment, and He that doeth righteousness at all times.

44) Nevertheless He regarded their affliction, when He heard their cry:

45) And He remembered for them His covenant, and repented according to the multitude of His mercies.

46) He made them also to be pitied of all those that carried them captives.

CHAPTER 107

1) O give thanks unto the Lord, for He is good: for His mercy endureth for ever.

2)   Let the redeemed of the Lord say so, whom He hath redeemed from the hand of the enemy;

3)   And gathered them out of the lands, from the east, and from the west, from the north, and from the south.

4)   They wandered in the wilderness in a solitary way; they found no city to dwell in.

5)   Hungry and thirsty, their soul fainted in them.

6)   Then they cried unto the Lord in their trouble, and He delivered them out of their distresses.

7)   And He led them forth by the right way, that they might go to a city of habitation.

8)   Oh that men would praise the Lord for His goodness, and for His wonderful works to the children of men!

9)   For He satisfieth the longing soul, and filleth the hungry soul with goodness.

10)   Such as sit in darkness and in the shadow of death, being bound in affliction and iron;

13)   Then they cried unto the Lord in their trouble, and He saved them out of their distresses.

14)   He brought them out of darkness and the shadow of death, and brake their bands in sunder.

15)   Oh that men would praise the Lord for His goodness, and for His wonderful works to the children of men!

16)   For He hath broken the gates of brass, and cut the bars of iron in sunder.

19)   Then they cry unto the Lord in their trouble, and He saveth them out of their distresses.

20)   He sent His word, and healed them, and

delivered them from their destructions.

21) Oh that men would praise the Lord for His goodness, and for His wonderful works to the children of men!

22) And let them sacrifice the sacrifices of thanksgiving, and declare His works with rejoicing.

23) They that go down to the sea in ships, that do business in great waters;

24) These see the works of the Lord, and His wonders in the deep.

25) For He commandeth, and raiseth the stormy wind, which lifteth up the waves thereof.

26) They mount up to the Heaven, they go down again to the depths: their soul is melted because of trouble.

27) They reel to and fro, and stagger like a drunken man, and are at their wit's end.

28) Then they cry unto the Lord in their trouble, and He bringeth them out of their distresses.

29) He maketh the storm a calm, so that the waves thereof are still.

30) Then are they glad because they be quiet; so He bringeth them unto their desired heaven.

31) Oh that men would praise the Lord for His goodness, and for His wonderful works to the children of men!

32) Let them exalt Him also in the congregation of the people, and praise Him in the assembly of the elders.

41) Yet setteth He the poor on high from affliction, and maketh Him families like a flock.

42) The righteous shall see it, and rejoice: and all iniquity shall stop her mouth.

43) Whoso is wise, and will observe these things, even they shall understand the lovingkindness of the Lord.

CHAPTER 108

13) Through God we shall do valiantly: for He it is that shall tread down our enemies.

CHAPTER 109

31) For He shall stand at the right hand of the poor, to save him from those that condemn his soul.

CHAPTER 111

2) The works of the Lord are great, sought out of all them that have pleasure therein.

3) His work is honourable and glorious: and His righteousness endureth for ever.

4) He hath made His wonderful works to be remembered: the Lord is gracious and full of compassion.

5) He hath given meat unto them that fear Him: He will ever be mindful of His covenant.

6) He hath shewed His people the power of His works, that He may give them the heritage of the heathen.

7) The works of His hands are verity and judgment; all His commandments are sure.

8) They stand fast for ever and ever, and are done in truth and uprightness.

9) He sent redemption unto His people: He hath commanded His covenant for ever: holy and reverend is His name.

10) The fear of the Lord is the beginning of

Wisdom: a good understanding have all they that do His commandments: His praise endureth for ever.

CHAPTER 112

1)   Praise ye the Lord. Blessed is the man that feareth the Lord, that delighteth grcatly in His commandments.

2)   His Seed shall be mighty upon earth: the generation of the upright shall be blessed.

3)   Wealth and riches shall be in his house: and his righteousness endureth for ever.

4)   Unto the upright there ariseth light in the darkness: He is gracious, and full of compassion, and righteous.

7)   He shall not be afraid of evil tidings: His heart is fixed, trusting in the Lord.

8)   His heart is established, he shall not be afraid, until he see his desire upon his enemies.

9)   He hath dispersed, he hath given to the poor; his righteousness endureth for ever; his horn shall be exalted with honour.

CHAPTER 113

5)   Who is like unto the Lord our God, who dwelleth on high,

7)   He raiseth up the poor out of the dust, and lifteth the needy out of the dunghill;

8)   That He may set him with princes, even with the princes of His people.

9)   He maketh the barren woman to keep house, and to be a joyful mother of children. Praise ye the Lord.

CHAPTER 115

9) O Israel, trust thou in the Lord: He is their help and their shield.

11) Ye that fear the Lord, trust in the Lord: He is their help and their shield.

12) The Lord hath been mindful of us: He will bless us; He will bless the house of Israel; He will bless the house of Aaron.

13) He will bless them that fear the Lord, both small and great.

14) The Lord shall increase you more and more, you and your children.

15) Ye are blessed of the Lord which made Heaven and earth.

16) The Heaven, even the Heavens, are the Lord's: but the earth hath He given to the children of men.

CHAPTER 116

6) The Lord preserveth the simple: I was brought low, and He helped me.

7) Return unto thy rest, O my soul; for the Lord hath dealt bountifully with thee.

8) For thou hast delivered my soul from death, mine eyes from tears, and my feet from falling.

CHAPTER 118

5) I called upon the Lord in distress: the Lord answered me, and set me in a large place.

6) The Lord is on my side; I will not fear: what can man do unto me?

7) The Lord taketh my part with them that help me: therefore shall I see my desire upon them that

hate me.

8)   It is better to trust in the Lord than to put confidence in man.

9)   It is better to trust in the Lord than to put confidence in princes.

13) Thou hast thrust sore at me that I might fall: but the Lord helped me.

14) The Lord is my strength and song, and is become my salvation.

15) The voice of rejoicing and salvation is in the tabernacles of the righteous: the right hand of the Lord doeth valiantly.

16) The right hand of the Lord is exalted: the right hand of the Lord doeth valiantly.

17) I shall not die, but live, and declare the works of the Lord.

21) I will praise thee: for thou hast heard me, and art become my salvation.

23) This is the Lord's doing, it is marvellous in our eyes.

24) This is the day which the Lord hath made; we will rejoice and be glad in it.

25) Save now, I beseech Thee, O Lord: O Lord, I beseech Thee, send now prosperity.

CHAPTER 119

1)   Blessed are the undefiled in the way, who walk in the law of the Lord.

2)   Blessed are they that keep His testimonies, and that seek Him with the whole heart.

9)   Wherewithal shall a young man cleanse his way? by taking heed thereto according to Thy word.

45) And I will walk at liberty: for I seek Thy

precepts.

50) This is my comfort in my affliction: for Thy word hath quickened me.

68) Thou art good, and doest good; teach me Thy statutes.

72) The law of Thy mouth is better unto me than thousands of gold and silver.

98) Thou through Thy commandments hast made me wiser than mine enemies: for they are ever with me.

99) I have more understanding than all my teachers: for Thy testimonies are my meditation.

100) I understand more than the ancients, because I keep Thy precepts.

101) I have refrained my feet from every evil way, that I might keep Thy word.

103) How sweet are Thy words unto my taste! yea, sweeter than honey to my mouth!

104) Through Thy precepts I get understanding: therefore I hate every false way.

130) The entrance of Thy words giveth light; it giveth understanding unto the simple.

156) Great are Thy tender mercies, O Lord: quicken me according to Thy judgments.

165) Great peace have they which love Thy law: and nothing shall offend them.

CHAPTER 121

1) I will lift up mine eyes unto the hills, from whence cometh my help.

2) My help cometh from the Lord, which made Heaven and earth.

3) He will not suffer thy foot to be moved: He that keepeth thee will not slumber.

4)   Behold, He that keepeth Israel shall neither slumber nor sleep.

5)   The Lord is thy keeper: the Lord is thy shade upon thy right hand.

6)   The sun shall not smite thee by day, nor the moon by night.

7)   The Lord shall preserve thee from all evil: He shall preserve thy soul.

8)   The Lord shall preserve thy going out and thy coming in from this time forth, and even for evermore.

CHAPTER 122

1)   I was glad when they said unto me, Let us go into the house of the Lord.

6)   Pray for the peace of Jerusalem: they shall prosper that love thee.

7)   Peace be within thy walls, and prosperity within thy palaces.

8)   For my brethren and companions' sakes, I will now say, Peace be within thee.

CHAPTER 124

1)   If it had not been the Lord who was on our side, now may Israel say;

2)   If it had not been the Lord who was on our side, when men rose up against us:

3)   Then they had swallowed us up quick, when their wrath was kindled against us:

4)   Then the waters had overwhelmed us, the stream had gone over our soul:

5)   Then the proud waters had gone over our soul.

6)   Blessed be the Lord, who hath not given us as a prey to their teeth.

7)   Our soul is escaped as a bird out of the snare of the fowlers: the snare is broken, and we are escaped.

8)   Our help is in the name of the Lord, who made Heaven and earth.

CHAPTER 125

1)   They that trust in the Lord shall be as mount Zion, which cannot be removed, but abideth for ever.

2)   As the mountains are round about Jerusalem, so the Lord is round about His people from henceforth even for ever.

3)   For the rod of the wicked shall not rest upon the lot of the righteous; lest the righteous put forth their hands unto iniquity.

CHAPTER 126

1)   When the Lord turned again the captivity of Zion, we were like them that dream.

2)   Then was our mouth filled with laughter, and our tongue with singing: then said they among the heathen, The Lord hath done great things for them.

3)   The Lord hath done great things for us; whereof we are glad.

4)   Turn again our captivity, O Lord, as the streams in the south.

5)   They that sow in tears shall reap in joy.

6)   He that goeth forth and weepeth, bearing precious Seed, shall doubtless come again with rejoicing, bringing his sheaves with him.

CHAPTER 127

2)   It is vain for you to rise up early, to sit up late, to eat the bread of sorrows: for so He giveth His beloved sleep.

3)   Lo, children are an heritage of the Lord and the fruit of the womb is His reward.

4)   As arrows are in the hand of a mighty man; so are children of the youth.

5)   Happy is the man that hath his quiver full of them: they shall not be ashamed, but they shall speak with the enemies in the gate.

CHAPTER 128

1)   Blessed is every one that feareth the Lord; that walketh in His ways.

2)   For thou shalt eat the labour of thine hands: happy shalt thou be, and it shall be well with thee.

3)   Thy wife shall be as a fruitful vine by the sides of thine house: thy children like olive plants round about thy table.

4)   Behold, that thus shall the man be blessed that feareth the Lord.

5)   The Lord shall bless thee out of Zion: and thou shalt see the good of Jerusalem all the days of thy life.

6)   Yea, thou shalt see thy children's children, and peace upon Israel.

CHAPTER 130

3)   If Thou, Lord, shouldest mark iniquities, O Lord, who shall stand?

4)   But there is forgiveness with Thee, that Thou mayest be feared.

19) Sihon king of the Amorites: for His mercy endureth for ever:

20) And Og the king of Bashan: for His mercy endureth for ever:

21) And gave their land for an heritage: for His mercy endureth for ever:

22) Even an heritage unto Israel His servant: for His mercy endureth for ever.

23) Who remembered us in our low estate: for His mercy endureth for ever:

24) And hath redeemed us from our enemies: for His mercy endureth for ever.

25) Who giveth food to all flesh: for His mercy endureth for ever.

26) O give thanks unto the God of Heaven: for His mercy endureth for ever.

CHAPTER 138

3) In the day when I cried Thou answeredst me, and strengthenedst me with strength in my soul.

7) Though I walk in the midst of trouble, Thou wilt revive me: Thou shalt stretch forth Thine hand against the wrath of mine enemies, and Thy right hand shall save me.

8) The Lord will perfect that which concerneth me: Thy mercy, O Lord, endureth for ever: forsake not the works of Thine own hands.

CHAPTER 139

1) O Lord, Thou hast searched me, and known me.

2) Thou knowest my downsitting and mine uprising, Thou understandest my thought afar off.

3) Thou compassest my path and my lying down, and art acquainted with all my ways.

4) For there is not a word in my tongue, but, lo, O Lord, Thou knowest it altogether.

5) Thou hast beset me behind and before, and laid Thine hand upon me.

6) Such knowledge is too wonderful for me; it is high, I cannot attain unto it.

7) Whither shall I go from Thy Spirit? or whither shall I flee from Thy Presence?

8) If I ascend up into Heaven, Thou art there: if I make my bed in hell, behold, Thou art there.

9) If I take the wings of the morning, and dwell in the uttermost parts of the sea;

10) Even there shall Thy hand lead me, and Thy right hand shall hold me.

11) If I say, Surely the darkness shall cover me; even the night shall be light about me.

12) Yea, the darkness hideth not from thee; but the night shineth as the day: the darkness and the light are both alike to Thee.

13) For Thou hast possessed my reins: Thou hast covered me in my mother's womb.

14) I will praise thee; for I am fearfully and wonderfully made: marvellous are Thy works; and that my soul knoweth right well.

15) My substance was not hid from Thee, when I was made in secret, and curiously wrought in the lowest parts of the earth.

16) Thine eyes did see my substance, yet being unperfect; and in Thy book all my members were written, which in continuance were fashioned, when as yet there was none of them.

17) How precious also are Thy thoughts unto

me, O God! how great is the sum of them!

18) If I should count them, they are more in number than the sand: when I awake, I am still with Thee.

CHAPTER 140

7) O God the Lord, the strength of my salvation, Thou hast covered my head in the day of battle.

12) I know that the Lord will maintain the cause of the afflicted, and the right of the poor.

13) Surely the righteous shall give thanks unto Thy name: the upright shall dwell in Thy presence.

CHAPTER 142

7) Bring my soul out of prison, that I may praise Thy name: the righteous shall compass me about; for Thou shalt deal bountifully with me.

CHAPTER 144

1) Blessed be the Lord my strength, which teacheth my hands to war, and my fingers to fight:

2) My goodness, and my fortress; my high tower, and my deliverer; my shield, and He in whom I trust; Who subdueth my people under me.

CHAPTER 145

8) The Lord is gracious, and full of compassion; slow to anger, and of great mercy.

9) The Lord is good to all: and His tender mercies are over all His works.

10) All Thy works shall praise Thee, O Lord; and Thy saints shall bless Thee.

11) They shall speak of the glory of Thy kingdom, and talk of Thy power;

12) To make known to the sons of men His mighty acts, and the glorious majesty of His kingdom.

13) Thy kingdom is an everlasting kingdom, and Thy dominion endureth throughout all generations.

14) The Lord upholdeth all that fall, and raiseth up all those that be bowed down.

15) The eyes of all wait upon Thee; and Thou givest them their meat in due season.

16) Thou openest Thine hand, and satisfiest the desire of every living thing.

17) The Lord is righteous in all His ways, and holy in all His works.

18) The Lord is nigh unto all them that call upon Him, to all that call upon Him in truth.

19) He will fulfil the desire of them that fear Him: He also will hear their cry, and will save them.

20) The Lord preserveth all them that love Him: but all the wicked will He destroy.

CHAPTER 146

5) Happy is he that hath the God of Jacob for his help, whose hope is in the Lord his God:

6) Which made Heaven, and earth, the sea, and all that therein is: which keepeth truth for ever:

7) Which executeth judgment for the oppressed: which giveth food to the hungry. The Lord looseth the prisoners:

8) The Lord openeth the eyes of the blind: the Lord raiseth them that are bowed down: the Lord loveth the righteous:

9) The Lord preserveth the strangers; He relieveth the fatherless and widow: but the way of the wicked He turneth upside down.

CHAPTER 147

2) The Lord doth build up Jerusalem: He gathereth together the outcasts of Israel.

3) He healeth the broken in heart, and bindeth up their wounds.

4) He telleth the number of the stars; He calleth them all by their names.

5) Great is our Lord, and of great power: His understanding is infinite.

6) The Lord lifteth up the meek: He casteth the wicked down to the ground.

11) The Lord taketh pleasure in them that fear Him, in those that hope in His mercy.

12) Praise the Lord, O Jerusalem; praise thy God, O Zion.

13) For He hath strengthened the bars of thy gates; He hath blessed thy children within thee.

14) He maketh peace in thy borders, and filleth thee with the finest of the wheat.

CHAPTER 149

4) For the Lord taketh pleasure in His people: He will beautify the meek with salvation.

PROVERBS

CHAPTER 1

33) But whoso hearkeneth unto me shall dwell

safely, and shall be quiet from fear of evil.

CHAPTER 2

3)   Yea, if thou criest after knowledge, and liftest up thy voice for understanding;

4)   If thou seekest her as silver, and searchest for her as for hid treasures;

5)   Then shalt thou understand the fear of the Lord, and find the knowledge of God.

6)   For the Lord giveth Wisdom: out of His mouth cometh knowledge and understanding.

7)   He layeth up sound Wisdom for the righteous: He is a buckler to them that walk uprightly.

8)   He keepeth the paths of judgment, and preserveth the way of His saints.

9)   Then shalt thou understand righteousness, and judgment, and equity; yea, every good path.

10)   When Wisdom entereth into thine heart, and knowledge is pleasant unto thy soul;

11)   Discretion shall preserve thee, understanding shall keep thee:

12)   To deliver thee from the way of the evil man, from the man that speaketh froward things;

16)   To deliver thee from the strange woman, even from the stranger which flattereth with her words;

20)   That thou mayest walk in the way of good men, and keep the paths of the righteous.

21)   For the upright shall dwell in the land, and the perfect shall remain in it.

CHAPTER 3

1) My son, forget not My law; but let thine heart keep My commandments;

2) For length of days, and long life, and peace, shall they add to thee.

3) Let not mercy and truth forsake thee: bind them about thy neck; write them upon the table of thine heart:

4) So shalt thou find favour and good understanding in the sight of God and man.

5) Trust in the Lord with all thine heart; and lean not unto thine own understanding.

6) In all thy ways acknowledge Him, and He shall direct thy paths.

7) Be not wise in thine own eyes: fear the Lord, and depart from evil.

8) It shall be health to thy navel, and marrow to thy bones.

9) Honour the Lord with thy substance, and with the firstfruits of all thine increase:

10) So shall thy barns be filled with plenty, and thy presses shall burst out with new wine.

13) Happy is the man that findeth Wisdom, and the man that getteth understanding.

14) For the merchandise of it is better than the merchandise of silver, and the gain thereof than fine gold.

15) She is more precious than rubies: and all the things thou canst desire are not to be compared unto her.

16) Length of days is in her right hand; and in her left hand riches and honour.

17) Her ways are ways of pleasantness, and all her paths are peace.

18) She is a tree of life to them that lay hold upon her: and happy is every one that retaineth her.

21) My son, let not them depart from thine eyes: keep sound Wisdom and discretion:

22) So shall they be life unto thy soul, and grace to thy neck.

23) Then shalt thou walk in thy way safely, and thy foot shall not stumble.

24) When thou liest down, thou shalt not be afraid: yea, thou shalt lie down, and thy sleep shall be sweet.

25) Be not afraid of sudden fear, neither of the desolation of the wicked, when it cometh.

26) For the Lord shall be thy confidence, and shall keep thy foot from being taken.

33) The curse of the Lord is in the house of the wicked: but He blesseth the habitation of the just.

35) The wise shall inherit glory: but shame shall be the promotion of fools.

CHAPTER 4

7) Wisdom is the principal thing; therefore get Wisdom: and with all thy getting get understanding.

8) Exalt her, and she shall promote thee: she shall bring thee to honour, when thou dost embrace her.

9) She shall give to thine head an ornament of grace: a crown of glory shall she deliver to thee.

11) I have taught thee in the way of Wisdom; I have led thee in right paths.

12) When thou goest, thy steps shall not be straitened; and when thou runnest, thou shalt not stumble.

13) Take fast hold of instruction; let her not go: keep her; for she is thy life.

18) But the path of the just is as the shining light, that shineth more and more unto the perfect day.

CHAPTER 6

20) My son, keep thy father's commandment, and forsake not the law of thy mother:

21) Bind them continually upon thine heart, and tie them about thy neck.

22) When thou goest, it shall lead thee; when thou sleepest, it shall keep thee; and when thou awakest, it shall talk with thee.

23) For the commandment is a lamp; and the law is light; and reproofs of instruction are the way of life:

24) To keep thee from the evil woman, from the flattery of the tongue of a strange woman.

CHAPTER 7

3) Bind them upon thy fingers, write them upon the table of thine heart.

4) Say unto Wisdom, Thou art my sister; and call understanding thy kinswoman:

CHAPTER 8

11) For Wisdom is better than rubies; and all the things that may be desired are not to be compared to it.

14) Counsel is mine, and sound Wisdom: I am understanding; I have strength.

15) By Me kings reign, and princes decree justice.

16) By Me princes rule, and nobles, even all the judges of the earth.

17) I love them that love Me; and those that seek me early shall find me.

18) Riches and honour are with Me; yea, durable riches and righteousness.

19) My fruit is better than gold, yea, than fine gold; and my revenue than choice silver.

20) I lead in the way of righteousness, in the midst of the paths of judgment:

21) That I may cause those that love Me to inherit substance; and I will fill their treasures.

34) Blessed is the man that heareth Me, watching daily at My gates, waiting at the posts of My doors.

35) For whoso findeth Me findeth life, and shall obtain favour of the Lord.

CHAPTER 9

10) The fear of the Lord is the beginning of Wisdom: and the knowledge of the holy is understanding.

11) For by Me thy days shall be multiplied, and the years of thy life shall be increased.

CHAPTER 10

3) The Lord will not suffer the soul of the righteous to famish: but He casteth away the substance of the wicked.

4) He becometh poor that dealeth with a slack

hand: but the hand of the diligent maketh rich.

5) He that gathereth in summer is a wise son: but he that sleepeth in harvest is a son that causeth shame.

6) Blessings are upon the head of the just: but violence covereth the mouth of the wicked.

16) The labour of the righteous tendeth to life: the fruit of the wicked to sin.

17) He is in the way of life that keepeth instruction: but he that refuseth reproof erreth.

22) The blessing of the Lord, it maketh rich, and he addeth no sorrow with it.

24) The fear of the wicked, it shall come upon him: but the desire of the righteous shall be granted.

27) The fear of the Lord prolongeth days: but the years of the wicked shall be shortened.

28) The hope of the righteous shall be gladness: but the expectation of the wicked shall perish.

29) The way of the Lord is strength to the upright: but destruction shall be to the workers of iniquity.

30) The righteous shall never be removed: but the wicked shall not inhabit the earth.

31) The mouth of the just bringeth forth Wisdom: but the froward tongue shall be cut out.

32) The lips of the righteous know what is acceptable: but the mouth of the wicked speaketh frowardness.

CHAPTER 11

3) The integrity of the upright shall guide them: but the perverseness of transgressors shall destroy them.

8) The righteous is delivered out of trouble, and

the wicked cometh in his stead.

11) By the blessing of the upright the city is exalted: but it is overthrown by the mouth of the wicked.

14) Where no counsel is, the people fall: but in the multitude of counsellors there is safcty.

16) A gracious woman retaineth honour: and strong men retain riches.

17) The merciful man doeth good to his own soul: but he that is cruel troubleth his own flesh.

21) Though hand join in hand, the wicked shall not be unpunished: but the Seed of the righteous shall be delivered.

24) There is that scattereth, and yet increaseth; and there is that withholdeth more than is meet, but it tendcth to poverty.

25) The liberal soul shall be made fat: and he that watereth shall be watered also himself.

26) He that withholdeth corn, the people shall curse him: but blessing shall be upon the head of him that selleth it.

28) He that trusteth in his riches shall fall: but the righteous shall flourish as a branch.

30) The fruit of the righteous is a tree of life; and he that winneth souls is wise.

CHAPTER 12

2) A good man obtaineth favour of the Lord: but a man of wicked devices will He condemn.

11) He that tilleth his land shall be satisfied with bread: but he that followeth vain persons is void of understanding.

12) The wicked desireth the net of evil men: but

the root of the righteous yieldeth fruit.

13) The wicked is snared by the transgression of his lips: but the just shall come out of trouble.

14) A man shall be satisfied with good by the fruit of his mouth: and the recompence of a man's hands shall be rendered unto him.

18) There is that speaketh like the piercings of a sword: but the tongue of the wise is health.

24) The hand of the diligent shall bear rule: but the slothful shall be under tribute.

CHAPTER 13

3) He that keepeth his mouth keepeth his life: but he that openeth wide his lips shall have destruction.

4) The soul of the sluggard desireth, and hath nothing: but the soul of the diligent shall be made fat.

7) There is that maketh himself rich, yet hath nothing: there is that maketh himself poor, yet hath great riches.

11) Wealth gotten by vanity shall be diminished: but he that gathereth by labour shall increase.

15) Good understanding giveth favour: but the way of transgressors is hard.

18) Poverty and shame shall be to him that refuseth instruction: but he that regardeth reproof shall be honoured.

20) He that walketh with wise men shall be wise: but a companion of fools shall be destroyed.

25) The righteous eateth to the satisfying of his soul: but the belly of the wicked shall want.

CHAPTER 14

26) In the fear of the Lord is strong confidence: and His children shall have a place of refuge.

27) The fear of the Lord is a fountain of life, to depart from the snares of death.

34) Righteousness exalteth a nation: but sin is a reproach to any people.

CHAPTER 15

6) In the house of the righteous is much treasure: but in the revenues of the wicked is trouble.

29) The Lord is far from the wicked: but He heareth the prayer of the righteous.

CHAPTER 16

3) Commit thy works unto the Lord, and thy thoughts shall be established.

7) When a man's ways please the Lord, He maketh even his enemies to be at peace with him.

15) In the light of the king's countenance is life; and his favour is as a cloud of the latter rain.

20) He that handleth a matter wisely shall find good: and whoso trusteth in the Lord, happy is he.

CHAPTER 18

10) The name of the Lord is a strong tower: the righteous runneth into it, and is safe.

16) A man's gift maketh room for him, and bringeth him before great men.

21) Death and life are in the power of the tongue: and they that love it shall eat the fruit thereof.

22) Whoso findeth a wife findeth a good thing,

and obtaineth favour of the Lord.

24) A man that hath friends must shew himself friendly: and there is a friend that sticketh closer than a brother.

CHAPTER 19

14) House and riches are the inheritance of fathers: and a prudent wife is from the Lord.

17) He that hath pity upon the poor lendeth unto the Lord; and that which he hath given will He pay him again.

23) The fear of the Lord tendeth to life: and he that hath it shall abide satisfied; he shall not be visited with evil.

CHAPTER 20

27) The spirit of man is the candle of the Lord, searching all the inward parts of the belly.

CHAPTER 21

5) The thoughts of the diligent tend only to plenteousness; but of every one that is hasty only to want.

21) He that followeth after righteousness and mercy findeth life, righteousness, and honour.

CHAPTER 22

4) By humility and the fear of the Lord are riches, and honour, and life.

9) He that hath a bountiful eye shall be blessed; for he giveth of his bread to the poor.

11) He that loveth pureness of heart, for the

grace of his lips the king shall be his friend.

29) Seest thou a man diligent in his business? he shall stand before kings; he shall not stand before mean men.

CHAPTER 24

3) Through Wisdom is an house builded; and by understanding it is established:

4) And by knowledge shall the chambers be filled with all precious and pleasant riches.

5) A wise man is strong; yea, a man of knowledge increaseth strength.

6) For by wise counsel thou shalt make thy war: and in multitude of counsellors there is safety.

13) My son, eat thou honey, because it is good; and the honeycomb, which is sweet to thy taste:

14) So shall the knowledge of Wisdom be unto thy soul: when thou hast found it, then there shall be a reward, and thy expectation shall not be cut off.

16) For a just man falleth seven times, and riseth up again: but the wicked shall fall into mischief.

CHAPTER 28

5) Evil men understand not judgment: but they that seek the Lord understand all things.

10) Whoso causeth the righteous to go astray in an evil way, he shall fall himself into his own pit: but the upright shall have good things in possession.

13) He that covereth his sins shall not prosper: but whoso confesseth and forsaketh them shall have mercy.

18) Whoso walketh uprightly shall be saved: but he that is perverse in his ways shall fall at once.

19) He that tilleth his land shall have plenty of bread: but he that followeth after vain persons shall have poverty enough.

20) A faithful man shall abound with blessings: but he that maketh haste to be rich shall not be innocent.

27) He that giveth unto the poor shall not lack: but he that hideth his eyes shall have many a curse.

CHAPTER 29

25) The fear of man bringeth a snare: but whoso putteth his trust in the Lord shall be safe.

CHAPTER 30

5) Every word of God is pure: He is a shield unto them that put their trust in Him.

CHAPTER 31

11) The heart of her husband doth safely trust in her, so that he shall have no need of spoil.

12) She will do him good and not evil all the days of her life.

28) Her children arise up, and call her blessed; her husband also, and he praiseth her.

30) Favour is deceitful, and beauty is vain: but a woman that feareth the Lord, she shall be praised.

ECCLESIASTES

CHAPTER 2

26) For God giveth to a man that is good in His sight Wisdom, and knowledge, and joy: but to the sinner He giveth travail, to gather and to heap up, that He may give to him that is good before God. This also is vanity and vexation of spirit.

CHAPTER 3

11) He hath made every thing beautiful in His time: also He hath set the world in their heart, so that no man can find out the work that God maketh from the beginning to the end.

12) I know that there is no good in them, but for a man to rejoice, and to do good in his life.

13) And also that every man should eat and drink, and enjoy the good of all his labour, it is the gift of God.

CHAPTER 5

19) Every man also to whom God hath given riches and wealth, and hath given him power to eat thereof, and to take his portion, and to rejoice in his labour; this is the gift of God.

CHAPTER 7

12) For Wisdom is a defence, and money is a defence: but the excellency of knowledge is, that Wisdom giveth life to them that have it.

18) It is good that thou shouldest take hold of this; yea, also from this withdraw not thine hand: for he that feareth God shall come forth of them all.

19) Wisdom strengtheneth the wise more than ten mighty men which are in the city.

CHAPTER 11

1)   Cast thy bread upon the waters: for thou shalt find it after many days.

6)   In the morning sow thy Seed, and in the evening withhold not thine hand: for thou knowest not whether shall prosper, either this or that, or whether they both shall be alike good.

THE SONG OF SOLOMON

CHAPTER 2

3)   As the apple tree among the trees of the wood, so is my beloved among the sons. I sat down under His shadow with great delight, and His fruit was sweet to my taste.

4)   He brought me to the banqueting house, and His banner over me was love.

CHAPTER 7

10)   I am my beloved's, and His desire is toward me.

CHAPTER 8

7)   Many waters cannot quench love, neither can the floods drown it: if a man would give all the substance of his house for love, it would utterly be contemned.

ISAIAH

CHAPTER 1

18)   Come now, and let us reason together, saith

the Lord: though your sins be as scarlet, they shall be as white as snow; though they be red like crimson, they shall be as wool.

19) If ye be willing and obedient, ye shall eat the good of the land:

CHAPTER 10

27) And it shall come to pass in that day, that his burden shall be taken away from off thy shoulder, and his yoke from off thy neck, and the yoke shall be destroyed because of the anointing.

CHAPTER 11

1)   And there shall come forth a rod out of the stem of Jesse, and a Branch shall grow out of his roots:

2)   And the spirit of the Lord shall rest upon him, the spirit of Wisdom and understanding, the spirit of counsel and might, the spirit of knowledge and of the fear of the Lord;

3)   And shall make him of quick understanding in the fear of the Lord: and he shall not judge after the sight of his eyes, neither reprove after the hearing of his ears:

4)   But with righteousness shall He judge the poor, and reprove with equity for the meek of the earth: and He shall smite the earth with the rod of His mouth, and with the breath of His lips shall He slay the wicked.

5)   And righteousness shall be the girdle of His loins, and faithfulness the girdle of His reins.

6)   The wolf also shall dwell with the lamb, and the leopard shall lie down with the kid; and the calf and the young lion and the fatling together; and a little child shall lead them.

7)   And the cow and the bear shall feed; their young ones shall lie down together: and the lion shall eat straw like the ox.

8)   And the sucking child shall play on the hole of the asp, and the weaned child shall put his hand on the cockatrice's den.

9)   They shall not hurt nor destroy in all my holy mountain: for the earth shall be full of the knowledge of the Lord, as the waters cover the sea.

10)   And in that day there shall be a root of Jesse, which shall stand for an ensign of the people; to it shall the Gentiles seek: and His rest shall be glorious.

CHAPTER 12

2)   Behold, God is my salvation; I will trust, and not be afraid: for the Lord Jehovah is my strength and my song; He also is become my salvation.

3)   Therefore with joy shall ye draw water out of the wells of salvation.

CHAPTER 14

3)   And it shall come to pass in the day that the Lord shall give thee rest from thy sorrow, and from thy fear, and from the hard bondage wherein thou wast made to serve,

5)   The Lord hath broken the staff of the wicked, and the sceptre of the rulers.

CHAPTER 25

1) O Lord, Thou art my God; I will exalt Thee, I will praise Thy name; for Thou hast done wonderful things; Thy counsels of old are faithfulness and truth.

4) For Thou hast been a strength to the poor, a strength to the needy in his distress, a refuge from the storm, a shadow from the heat, when the blast of the terrible ones is as a storm against the wall.

8) He will swallow up death in victory; and the Lord God will wipe away tears from off all faces; and the rebuke of His people shall He take away from off all the earth: for the Lord hath spoken it.

9) And it shall be said in that day, Lo, this is our God; we have waited for Him, and He will save us: this is the Lord; we have waited for Him, we will be glad and rejoice in His salvation.

CHAPTER 26

3) Thou wilt keep him in perfect peace, whose mind is stayed on Thee: because he trusteth in Thee.

4) Trust ye in the Lord for ever: for in the Lord Jehovah is everlasting strength:

12) Lord, thou wilt ordain peace for us: for Thou also hast wrought all our works in us.

CHAPTER 29

18) And in that day shall the deaf hear the words of the book, and the eyes of the blind shall see out of obscurity, and out of darkness.

19) The meek also shall increase their joy in the

Lord, and the poor among men shall rejoice in the Holy One of Israel.

CHAPTER 30

21) And thine ears shall hear a word behind thee, saying, This is the way, walk ye in it, when ye turn to the right hand, and when ye turn to the left.

23) Then shall He give the rain of thy Seed, that thou shalt sow the ground withal; and bread of the increase of the earth, and it shall be fat and plenteous: in that day shall thy cattle feed in large pastures.

26) Moreover the light of the moon shall be as the light of the sun, and the light of the sun shall be sevenfold, as the light of seven days, in the day that the Lord bindeth up the breach of His people, and healeth the stroke of their wound.

CHAPTER 32

1) Behold, a king shall reign in righteousness, and princes shall rule in judgment.

2) And a man shall be as an hiding place from the wind, and a covert from the tempest; as rivers of water in a dry place, as the shadow of a great rock in a weary land.

3) And the eyes of them that see shall not be dim, and the ears of them that hear shall hearken.

4) The heart also of the rash shall understand knowledge, and the tongue of the stammerers shall be ready to speak plainly.

17) And the work of righteousness shall be peace; and the effect of righteousness quietness and

assurance for ever.

18) And My people shall dwell in a peaceable habitation, and in sure dwellings, and in quiet resting places;

CHAPTER 33

6) And Wisdom and knowledge shall be the stability of thy times, and strength of salvation: the fear of the Lord is his treasure.

15) He that walketh righteously, and speaketh uprightly; he that despiseth the gain of oppressions, that shaketh his hands from holding of bribes, that stoppeth his ears from hearing of blood, and shutteth his eyes from seeing evil;

16) He shall dwell on high: his place of defence shall be the munitions of rocks: bread shall be given him; his waters shall be sure.

21) But there the glorious Lord will be unto us a place of broad rivers and streams; wherein shall go no galley with oars, neither shall gallant ship pass thereby.

22) For the Lord is our judge, the Lord is our lawgiver, the Lord is our king; He will save us.

CHAPTER 35

4) Say to them that are of a fearful heart, Be strong, fear not: behold, your God will come with vengeance, even God with a recompence; He will come and save you.

5) Then the eyes of the blind shall be opened, and the ears of the deaf shall be unstopped.

6) Then shall the lame man leap as an hart, and the tongue of the dumb sing: for in the

wilderness shall waters break out, and streams in the desert.

7)   And the parched ground shall become a pool, and the thirsty land springs of water: in the habitation of dragons, where each lay, shall be grass with reeds and rushes.

8)   And an highway shall be there, and a way, and it shall be called The way of holiness; the unclean shall not pass over it; but it shall be for those: the wayfaring men, though fools, shall not err therein.

9)   No lion shall be there, nor any ravenous beast shall go up thereon, it shall not be found there; but the redeemed shall walk there:

10) And the ransomed of the Lord shall return, and come to Zion with songs and everlasting joy upon their heads: they shall obtain joy and gladness, and sorrow and sighing shall flee away.

CHAPTER 40

3)   The voice of him that crieth in the wilderness, Prepare ye the way of the Lord, make straight in the desert a highway for our God.

4)   Every valley shall be exalted, and every mountain and hill shall be made low: and the crooked shall be made straight, and the rough places plain:

5)   And the glory of the Lord shall be revealed, and all flesh shall see it together: for the mouth of the Lord hath spoken it.

10) Behold, the Lord God will come with strong hand, and His arm shall rule for Him: behold, His reward is with Him, and His work before him.

11) He shall feed His flock like a shepherd: He

shall gather the lambs with His arm, and carry them in His bosom, and shall gently lead those that are with young.

26) Lift up your eyes on high, and behold who hath created these things, that bringeth out their host by number: He calleth them all by names by the greatness of His might, for that He is strong in power; not one faileth.

28) Hast thou not known? hast thou not heard, that the everlasting God, the Lord, the Creator of the ends of the earth, fainteth not, neither is weary? there is no searching of His understanding.

29) He giveth power to the faint; and to them that have no might He increaseth strength.

30) Even the youths shall faint and be weary, and the young men shall utterly fall:

31) But they that wait upon the Lord shall renew their strength; they shall mount up with wings as eagles; they shall run, and not be weary; and they shall walk, and not faint.

CHAPTER 41

8) But thou, Israel, art My servant, Jacob whom I have chosen, the Seed of Abraham My friend.

10) Fear thou not; for I am with thee: be not dismayed; for I am thy God: I will strengthen thee; yea, I will help thee; yea, I will uphold thee with the right hand of My righteousness.

11) Behold, all they that were incensed against thee shall be ashamed and confounded: they shall be as nothing; and they that strive with thee shall perish.

12) Thou shalt seek them, and shalt not find

them, even them that contended with thee: they that war against thee shall be as nothing, and as a thing of nought.

13) For I the Lord thy God will hold thy right hand, saying unto thee, Fear not; I will help thee.

17) When the poor and needy seek water, and there is none, and their tongue faileth for thirst, I the Lord will hear them, I the God of Israel will not forsake them.

18) I will open rivers in high places, and fountains in the midst of the valleys: I will make the wilderness a pool of water, and the dry land springs of water.

CHAPTER 42

5) Thus saith God the Lord, He that created the Heavens, and stretched them out; He that spread forth the earth, and that which cometh out of it; He that giveth breath unto the people upon it, and spirit to them that walk therein:

6) I the Lord have called thee in righteousness, and will hold thine hand, and will keep thee, and give thee for a covenant of the people, for a light of the Gentiles;

7) To open the blind eyes, to bring out the prisoners from the prison, and them that sit in darkness out of the prison house.

8) I am the Lord: that is My name: and My glory will I not give to another, neither My praise to graven images.

9) Behold, the former things are come to pass, and new things do I declare: before they spring forth I tell you of them.

15) I will make waste mountains and hills, and dry up all their herbs; and I will make the rivers islands, and I will dry up the pools.

16) And I will bring the blind by a way that they knew not; I will lead them in paths that they have not known: I will make darkness light before them, and crooked things straight. These things will I do unto them, and not forsake them.

CHAPTER 43

1) But now thus saith the Lord that created thee, O Jacob, and He that formed thee, O Israel, Fear not: for I have redeemed thee, I have called thee by thy name; thou art Mine.

2) When thou passest through the waters, I will be with thee; and through the rivers, they shall not overflow thee: when thou walkest through the fire, thou shalt not be burned; neither shall the flame kindle upon thee.

5) Fear not: for I am with thee: I will bring thy Seed from the east, and gather thee from the west;

6) I will say to the north, Give up; and to the south, Keep not back: bring my sons from far, and my daughters from the ends of the earth;

7) Even every one that is called by My name: for I have created him for my glory, I have formed him; yea, I have made him.

16) Thus saith the Lord, which maketh a way in the sea, and a path in the mighty waters;

17) Which bringeth forth the chariot and horse, the army and the power; they shall lie down together, they shall not rise: they are extinct, they are

quenched as tow.

18) Remember ye not the former things, neither consider the things of old.

19) Behold, I will do a new thing; now it shall spring forth; shall ye not know it? I will even make a way in the wilderness, and rivers in the desert.

25) I, even I, am He that blotteth out thy transgressions for Mine own sake, and will not remember thy sins.

CHAPTER 44

3) For I will pour water upon Him that is thirsty, and floods upon the dry ground: I will pour My Spirit upon thy Seed, and My blessing upon thine offspring:

4) And they shall spring up as among the grass, as willows by the water courses.

8) Fear ye not, neither be afraid: have not I told thee from that time, and have declared it? ye are even My witnesses. Is there a God beside Me? yea, there is no God; I know not any.

22) I have blotted out, as a thick cloud, thy transgressions, and, as a cloud, thy sins: return unto Me; for I have redeemed thee.

CHAPTER 45

2) I will go before thee, and make the crooked places straight: I will break in pieces the gates of brass, and cut in sunder the bars of iron:

3) And I will give thee the treasures of darkness, and hidden riches of secret places, that thou mayest know that I, the Lord, which call thee by thy name, am the God of Israel.

11)   Thus saith the Lord, the Holy One of Israel, and His Maker, Ask Me of things to come concerning My sons, and concerning the work of My hands command ye Me.

22)   Look unto Me, and be ye saved, all the ends of the earth: for I am God, and there is none else.

23)   I have sworn by Myself, the word is gone out of My mouth in righteousness, and shall not return, That unto Me every knee shall bow, every tongue shall swear.

24)   Surely, shall one say, in the Lord have I righteousness and strength: even to Him shall men come; and all that are incensed against Him shall be ashamed.

CHAPTER 46

9)   Remember the former things of old: for I am God, and there is none else; I am God, and there is none like Me,

11)   Calling a ravenous bird from the east, the man that executeth My counsel from a far country: yea, I have spoken it, I will also bring it to pass; I have purposed it, I will also do it.

CHAPTER 48

15)   I, even I, have spoken; yea, I have called him: I have brought him, and he shall make his way prosperous.

16)   Come ye near unto Me, hear ye this; I have not spoken in secret from the beginning; from the time that it was, there am I: and now the Lord God, and His Spirit, hath sent Me.

17) Thus saith the Lord, thy Redeemer, the Holy One of Israel; I am the Lord thy God which teacheth thee to profit, which leadeth thee by the way that thou shouldest go.

18) O that thou hadst hearkened to my commandments! then had thy peace been as a river, and thy righteousness as the waves of the sea:

19) Thy Seed also had been as the sand, and the offspring of thy bowels like the gravel thereof; His name should not have been cut off nor destroyed from before Me.

CHAPTER 49

9) That thou mayest say to the prisoners, Go forth; to them that are in darkness, Shew yourselves. They shall feed in the ways, and their pastures shall be in all high places.

10) They shall not hunger nor thirst; neither shall the heat nor sun smite them: for He that hath mercy on them shall lead them, even by the springs of water shall He guide them.

11) And I will make all My mountains a way, and My highways shall be exalted.

15) Can a woman forget her sucking child, that she should not have compassion on the son of her womb? yea, they may forget, yet will I not forget thee.

16) Behold, I have graven thee upon the palms of My hands; thy walls are continually before Me.

CHAPTER 50

4) The Lord God hath given me the tongue of the learned, that I should know how to speak a word in season to him that is weary: He wakeneth morning by morning, He wakeneth mine ear to hear

as the learned.

7)   For the Lord God will help me; therefore shall I not be confounded: therefore have I set my face like a flint, and I know that I shall not be ashamed.

10) Who is among you that feareth the Lord, that obeyeth the voice of His servant, that walketh in darkness, and hath no light? let him trust in the name of the Lord, and stay upon his God.

CHAPTER 51

11) Therefore the redeemed of the Lord shall return, and come with singing unto Zion; and everlasting joy shall be upon their head: they shall obtain gladness and joy; and sorrow and mourning shall flee away.

CHAPTER 52

7)   How beautiful upon the mountains are the feet of him that bringeth good tidings, that publisheth peace; that bringeth good tidings of good, that publisheth salvation; that saith unto Zion, Thy God reigneth!

12) For ye shall not go out with haste, nor go by flight: for the Lord will go before you; and the God of Israel will be your rereward.

CHAPTER 53

4)   Surely He hath borne our griefs, and carried our sorrows: yet we did esteem Him stricken, smitten of God, and afflicted.

5)   But He was wounded for our transgressions, He was bruised for our iniquities: the chastisement

of our peace was upon Him; and with His stripes we are healed.

6)   All we like sheep have gone astray; we have turned every one to his own way; and the Lord hath laid on Him the iniquity of us all.

11) He shall see of the travail of His soul, and shall be satisfied: by His knowledge shall my righteous servant justify many; for He shall bear their iniquities.

12) Therefore will I divide Him a portion with the great, and He shall divide the spoil with the strong; because He hath poured out His soul unto death: and He was numbered with the transgressors; and He bare the sin of many, and made intercession for the transgressors.

CHAPTER 54

2)   Enlarge the place of thy tent, and let them stretch forth the curtains of thine habitations: spare not, lengthen thy cords, and strengthen thy stakes;

3)   For thou shalt break forth on the right hand and on the left; and thy Seed shall inherit the Gentiles, and make the desolate cities to be inhabited.

4)   Fear not; for thou shalt not be ashamed: neither be thou confounded; for thou shalt not be put to shame: for thou shalt forget the shame of thy youth, and shalt not remember the reproach of thy widowhood any more.

5)   For thy Maker is thine husband; the Lord of hosts is His name; and thy Redeemer the Holy One of Israel; The God of the whole earth shall He be called.

7)   For a small moment have I forsaken thee;

but with great mercies will I gather thee.

8)   In a little wrath I hid my face from thee for a moment; but with everlasting kindness will I have mercy on thee, saith the Lord thy Redeemer.

10) For the mountains shall depart, and the hills be removed; but My kindness shall not depart from thee, neither shall the covenant of My peace be removed, saith the Lord that hath mercy on thee.

13) And all thy children shall be taught of the Lord; and great shall be the peace of thy children.

14) In righteousness shalt thou be established: thou shalt be far from oppression; for thou shalt not fear: and from terror; for it shall not come near thee.

15) Behold, they shall surely gather together, but not by Me: whosoever shall gather together against thee shall fall for thy sake.

17) No weapon that is formed against thee shall prosper; and every tongue that shall rise against thee in judgment thou shalt condemn. This is the heritage of the servants of the Lord, and their righteousness is of Me, saith the Lord.

CHAPTER 55

1)   Ho, every one that thirsteth, come ye to the waters, and he that hath no money; come ye, buy, and eat; yea, come, buy wine and milk without money and without price.

3)   Incline your ear, and come unto Me: hear, and your soul shall live; and I will make an everlasting covenant with you, even the sure mercies of David.

6)   Seek ye the Lord while He may be found, call ye upon Him while He is near:

7)   Let the wicked forsake his way, and the unrighteous man his thoughts: and let him return unto the Lord, and He will have mercy upon him; and to our God, for He will abundantly pardon.

8)   For My thoughts are not your thoughts, neither are your ways My ways, saith the Lord.

9)   For as the Heavens are higher than the earth, so are My ways higher than your ways, and My thoughts than your thoughts.

10)   For as the rain cometh down, and the snow from Heaven, and returneth not thither, but watereth the earth, and maketh it bring forth and bud, that it may give Seed to the sower, and bread to the eater:

11)   So shall My word be that goeth forth out of My mouth: it shall not return unto Me void, but it shall accomplish that which I please, and it shall prosper in the thing whereto I sent it.

12)   For ye shall go out with joy, and be led forth with peace: the mountains and the hills shall break forth before you into singing, and all the trees of the field shall clap their hands.

13)   Instead of the thorn shall come up the fir tree, and instead of the brier shall come up the myrtle tree: and it shall be to the Lord for a name, for an everlasting sign that shall not be cut off.

CHAPTER 57

13)   When thou criest, let thy companies deliver thee; but the wind shall carry them all away; vanity shall take them: but he that putteth his trust in me shall possess the land, and shall inherit my holy mountain;

15)   For thus saith the high and lofty One that

inhabiteth eternity, whose name is Holy; I dwell in the high and holy place, with him also that is of a contrite and humble spirit, to revive the spirit of the humble, and to revive the heart of the contrite ones.

18) I have seen his ways, and will heal him: I will lead him also, and restore comforts unto him and to his mourners.

19) I create the fruit of the lips; Peace, peace to him that is far off, and to him that is near, saith the Lord; and I will heal him.

CHAPTER 58

6) Is not this the fast that I have chosen? to loose the bands of wickedness, to undo the heavy burdens, and to let the oppressed go free, and that ye break every yoke?

7) Is it not to deal thy bread to the hungry, and that thou bring the poor that are cast out to thy house? when thou seest the naked, that thou cover him; and that thou hide not thyself from thine own flesh?

8) Then shall thy light break forth as the morning, and thine health shall spring forth speedily: and thy righteousness shall go before thee; the glory of the Lord shall be thy rereward.

9) Then shalt thou call, and the Lord shall answer; thou shalt cry, and he shall say, Here I am. If thou take away from the midst of thee the yoke, the putting forth of the finger, and speaking vanity;

10) And if thou draw out thy soul to the hungry, and satisfy the afflicted soul; then shall thy light rise in obscurity, and thy darkness be as the noon day:

11) And the Lord shall guide thee continually,

and satisfy thy soul in drought, and make fat thy bones: and thou shalt be like a watered garden, and like a spring of water, whose waters fail not.

12) And they that shall be of thee shall build the old waste places: thou shalt raise up the foundations of many generations; and thou shalt be called, The repairer of the breach, The restorer of paths to dwell in.

13) If thou turn away thy foot from the sabbath, from doing thy pleasure on My holy day; and call the sabbath a delight, the holy of the Lord, honourable; and shalt honour Him, not doing thine own ways, nor finding thine own pleasure, nor speaking thine own words:

14) Then shalt thou delight thyself in the Lord; and I will cause thee to ride upon the high places of the earth, and feed thee with the heritage of Jacob thy father: for the mouth of the Lord hath spoken it.

CHAPTER 59

1)   Behold, the Lord's hand is not shortened, that it cannot save; neither His ear heavy, that it cannot hear:

19) So shall they fear the name of the Lord from the west, and His glory from the rising of the sun. When the enemy shall come in like a flood, the Spirit of the Lord shall lift up a standard against him.

20) And the Redeemer shall come to Zion, and unto them that turn from transgression in Jacob, saith the Lord.

21) As for me, this is My covenant with them, saith the Lord; My Spirit that is upon thee, and My

words which I have put in thy mouth, shall not depart out of thy mouth, nor out of the mouth of thy Seed, nor out of the mouth of thy Seed's Seed, saith the Lord, from henceforth and for ever.

CHAPTER 60

1) Arise, shine; for thy light is come, and the glory of the Lord is risen upon thee.

2) For, behold, the darkness shall cover the earth, and gross darkness the people: but the Lord shall arise upon thee, and His glory shall be seen upon thee.

3) And the Gentiles shall come to thy light, and kings to the brightness of thy rising.

4) Lift up thine eyes round about, and see: all they gather themselves together, they come to thee: thy sons shall come from far, and thy daughters shall be nursed at thy side.

5) Then thou shalt see, and flow together, and thine heart shall fear, and be enlarged; because the abundance of the sea shall be converted unto thee, the forces of the Gentiles shall come unto thee.

CHAPTER 61

1) The Spirit of the Lord God is upon me; because the Lord hath anointed me to preach good tidings unto the meek; He hath sent me to bind up the brokenhearted, to proclaim liberty to the captives, and the opening of the prison to them that are bound;

2) To proclaim the acceptable year of the Lord, and the day of vengeance of our God; to comfort all that mourn;

3)　To appoint unto them that mourn in Zion, to give unto them beauty for ashes, the oil of joy for mourning, the garment of praise for the spirit of heaviness; that they might be called trees of righteousness, the planting of the Lord, that He might be glorified.

4)　And they shall build the old wastes, they shall raise up the former desolations, and they shall repair the waste cities, the desolations of many generations.

5)　And strangers shall stand and feed your flocks, and the sons of the alien shall be your plowmen and your vinedressers.

6)　But ye shall be named the Priests of the Lord: men shall call you the Ministers of our God: ye shall eat the riches of the Gentiles, and in their glory shall ye boast yourselves.

9)　And their Seed shall be known among the Gentiles, and their offspring among the people: all that see them shall acknowledge them, that they are the Seed which the Lord hath blessed.

10)　I will greatly rejoice in the Lord, my soul shall be joyful in my God; for He hath clothed me with the garments of salvation, He hath covered me with the robe of righteousness, as a bridegroom decketh himself with ornaments, and as a bride adorneth herself with her jewels.

CHAPTER 63

7)　I will mention the lovingkindnesses of the Lord, and the praises of the Lord, according to all that the Lord hath bestowed on us, and the great goodness toward the house of Israel, which He hath bestowed on them according to His mercies, and according to the multitude of His lovingkindnesses.

8)   For He said, Surely they are My people, children that will not lie: so He was their Saviour.

9)   In all their affliction He was afflicted, and the angel of His presence saved them: in His love and in His pity He redeemed them; and He bare them, and carried them all the days of old.

CHAPTER 64

4)   For since the beginning of the world men have not heard, nor perceived by the ear, neither hath the eye seen, O God, beside thee, what He hath prepared for him that waiteth for Him.

6)   But we are all as an unclean thing, and all our righteousnesses are as filthy rags; and we all do fade as a leaf; and our iniquities, like the wind, have taken us away.

8)   But now, O Lord, Thou art our Father; we are the clay, and Thou our potter; and we all are the work of Thy hand.

CHAPTER 65

21) And they shall build houses, and inhabit them; and they shall plant vineyards, and eat the fruit of them.

22) They shall not build, and another inhabit; they shall not plant, and another eat: for as the days of a tree are the days of My people, and Mine elect shall long enjoy the work of their hands.

23) They shall not labour in vain, nor bring forth for trouble; for they are the Seed of the blessed of the Lord, and their offspring with them.

24) And it shall come to pass, that before they

call, I will answer; and while they are yet speaking, I will hear.

CHAPTER 66

2)   For all those things hath mine hand made, and all those things have been, saith the Lord: but to this man will I look, even to him that is poor and of a contrite spirit, and trembleth at My word.

JEREMIAH

CHAPTER 1

4)   Then the word of the Lord came unto me, saying,

5)   Before I formed thee in the belly I knew thee; and before thou camest forth out of the womb I sanctified thee, and I ordained thee a prophet unto the nations.

8)   Be not afraid of their faces: for I am with thee to deliver thee, saith the Lord.

9)   Then the Lord put forth His hand, and touched my mouth. And the Lord said unto me, Behold, I have put My words in thy mouth.

10)   See, I have this day set thee over the nations and over the kingdoms, to root out, and to pull down, and to destroy, and to throw down, to build, and to plant.

12)   Then said the Lord unto me, Thou hast well seen: for I will hasten My word to perform it.

19)   And they shall fight against thee; but they shall not prevail against thee; for I am with thee, saith the Lord, to deliver thee.

CHAPTER 9

24) But let him that glorieth glory in this, that he understandeth and knoweth Me, that I am the Lord which exercise lovingkindness, judgment, and righteousness, in the earth: for in these things I delight, saith the Lord.

CHAPTER 10

6) Forasmuch as there is none like unto Thee, O Lord; Thou art great, and Thy name is great in might.

CHAPTER 15

16) Thy words were found, and I did eat them; and Thy word was unto me the joy and rejoicing of mine heart: for I am called by Thy name, O Lord God of hosts.

19) Therefore thus saith the Lord, If thou return, then will I bring thee again, and thou shalt stand before Me: and if thou take forth the precious from the vile, thou shalt be as My mouth: let them return unto thee; but return not thou unto them.

20) And I will make thee unto this people a fenced brasen wall: and they shall fight against thee, but they shall not prevail against thee: for I am with thee to save thee and to deliver thee, saith the Lord.

21) And I will deliver thee out of the hand of the wicked, and I will redeem thee out of the hand of the terrible.

CHAPTER 17

7) Blessed is the man that trusteth in the Lord, and whose hope the Lord is.

8) For he shall be as a tree planted by the waters, and that spreadeth out her roots by the river, and shall not see when heat cometh, but her leaf shall be green; and shall not be careful in the year of drought, neither shall cease from yielding fruit.

14) Heal me, O Lord, and I shall be healed; save me, and I shall be saved: for Thou art my praise.

CHAPTER 23

3) And I will gather the remnant of My flock out of all countries whither I have driven them, and will bring them again to their folds; and they shall be fruitful and increase.

4) And I will set up shepherds over them which shall feed them: and they shall fear no more, nor be dismayed, neither shall they be lacking, saith the Lord.

CHAPTER 24

6) For I will set Mine eyes upon them for good, and I will bring them again to this land: and I will build them, and not pull them down; and I will plant them, and not pluck them up.

7) And I will give them an heart to know Me, that I am the Lord: and they shall be My people, and I will be their God: for they shall return unto Me with their whole heart.

CHAPTER 29

11) For I know the thoughts that I think toward you, saith the Lord, thoughts of peace, and not of evil, to give you an expected end.

12) Then shall ye call upon Me, and ye shall go and pray unto Me, and I will hearken unto you.

13) And ye shall seek Me, and find Me, when ye shall search for Me with all your heart.

CHAPTER 30

10) Therefore fear thou not, O my servant Jacob, saith the Lord; neither be dismayed, O Israel: for, lo, I will save thee from afar, and thy Seed from the land of their captivity; and Jacob shall return, and shall be in rest, and be quiet, and none shall make him afraid.

17) For I will restore health unto thee, and I will heal thee of thy wounds, saith the Lord; because they called thee an Outcast, saying, This is Zion, whom no man seeketh after.

CHAPTER 31

3) The Lord hath appeared of old unto me, saying, Yea, I have loved thee with an everlasting love: therefore with lovingkindness have I drawn thee.

10) Hear the word of the Lord, O ye nations, and declare it in the isles afar off, and say, He that scattered Israel will gather him, and keep him, as a shepherd doth his flock.

11) For the Lord hath redeemed Jacob, and ransomed him from the hand of him that was

stronger than he.

12) Therefore they shall come and sing in the height of Zion, and shall flow together to the goodness of the Lord, for wheat, and for wine, and for oil, and for the young of the flock and of the herd: and their soul shall be as a watered garden; and they shall not sorrow any more at all.

14) And I will satiate the soul of the priests with fatness, and My people shall be satisfied with My goodness, saith the Lord.

25) For I have satiated the weary soul, and I have replenished every sorrowful soul.

33) But this shall be the covenant that I will make with the house of Israel; After those days, saith the Lord, I will put My law in their inward parts, and write it in their hearts; and will be their God, and they shall be My people.

CHAPTER 32

17) Ah Lord God! behold, thou hast made the Heaven and the earth by Thy great power and stretched out arm, and there is nothing too hard for Thee:

18) Thou shewest lovingkindness unto thousands, and recompensest the iniquity of the fathers into the bosom of their children after them: the Great, the Mighty God, the Lord of hosts, is His name,

19) Great in counsel, and mighty in work: for Thine eyes are open upon all the ways of the sons of men: to give every one according to his ways, and according to the fruit of his doings:

27) Behold, I am the Lord, the God of all flesh: is there any thing too hard for Me?

37) Behold, I will gather them out of all countries, whither I have driven them in Mine anger, and in My fury, and in great wrath; and I will bring them again unto this place, and I will cause them to dwell safely:

38) And they shall be My people, and I will be their God:

39) And I will give them one heart, and one way, that they may fear Me for ever, for the good of them, and of their children after them:

40) And I will make an everlasting covenant with them, that I will not turn away from them, to do them good; but I will put My fear in their hearts, that they shall not depart from Me.

41) Yea, I will rejoice over them to do them good, and I will plant them in this land assuredly with My whole heart and with My whole soul.

CHAPTER 33

3) Call unto Me, and I will answer thee, and shew thee great and mighty things, which thou knowest not.

8) And I will cleanse them from all their iniquity, whereby they have sinned against Me; and I will pardon all their iniquities, whereby they have sinned, and whereby they have transgressed against Me.

14) Behold, the days come, saith the Lord, that I will perform that good thing which I have promised unto the house of Israel and to the house of Judah.

CHAPTER 39

17) But I will deliver thee in that day, saith the Lord: and thou shalt not be given into the hand of the men of whom thou art afraid.

18) For I will surely deliver thee, and thou shalt not fall by the sword, but thy life shall be for a prey unto thee: because thou hast put thy trust in Me, saith the Lord.

LAMENTATIONS

CHAPTER 3

22) It is of the Lord's mercies that we are not consumed, because His compassions fail not.

23) They are new every morning: great is Thy faithfulness.

24) The Lord is my portion, saith my soul; therefore will I hope in Him.

25) The Lord is good unto them that wait for Him, to the soul that seeketh Him.

26) It is good that a man should both hope and quietly wait for the salvation of the Lord.

58) O Lord, thou hast pleaded the causes of my soul; thou hast redeemed my life.

EZEKIEL

CHAPTER 16

62) And I will establish My covenant with thee; and thou shalt know that I am the Lord:

63) That thou mayest remember, and be

confounded, and never open thy mouth any more because of thy shame, when I am pacified toward thee for all that thou hast done, saith the Lord God.

CHAPTER 33

15) If the wicked restore the pledge, give again that he had robbed, walk in the statutes of life, without committing iniquity; he shall surely live, he shall not die.

16) None of his sins that he hath committed shall be mentioned unto him: he hath done that which is lawful and right; he shall surely live.

19) But if the wicked turn from his wickedness, and do that which is lawful and right, he shall live thereby.

CHAPTER 34

11) For thus saith the Lord God; Behold, I, even I, will both search My sheep, and seek them out.

12) As a shepherd seeketh out his flock in the day that he is among his sheep that are scattered; so will I seek out My sheep, and will deliver them out of all places where they have been scattered in the cloudy and dark day.

13) And I will bring them out from the people, and gather them from the countries, and will bring them to their own land, and feed them upon the mountains of Israel by the rivers, and in all the inhabited places of the country.

14) I will feed them in a good pasture, and upon the high mountains of Israel shall their fold be: there shall they lie in a good fold, and in a fat pasture shall they feed upon the mountains of Israel.

15) I will feed My flock, and I will cause them

to lie down, saith the Lord God.

16) I will seek that which was lost, and bring again that which was driven away, and will bind up that which was broken, and will strengthen that which was sick: but I will destroy the fat and the strong; I will feed them with judgment.

26) And I will make them and the places round about My hill a blessing; and I will cause the shower to come down in his season; there shall be showers of blessing.

27) And the tree of the field shall yield her fruit, and the earth shall yield her increase, and they shall be safe in their land, and shall know that I am the Lord, when I have broken the bands of their yoke, and delivered them out of the hand of those that served themselves of them.

CHAPTER 36

9)   For, behold, I am for you, and I will turn unto you, and ye shall be tilled and sown:

10) And I will multiply men upon you, all the house of Israel, even all of it: and the cities shall be inhabited, and the wastes shall be builded:

11) And I will multiply upon you man and beast; and they shall increase and bring fruit: and I will settle you after your old estates, and will do better unto you than at your beginnings: and ye shall know that I am the Lord.

25) Then will I sprinkle clean water upon you, and ye shall be clean: from all your filthiness, and from all your idols, will I cleanse you.

26) A new heart also will I give you, and a new spirit will I put within you: and I will take away the

stony heart out of your flesh, and I will give you an heart of flesh.

27) And I will put My Spirit within you, and cause you to walk in my statutes, and ye shall keep My judgments, and do them.

28) And ye shall dwell in the land that I gave to your fathers; and ye shall be My people, and I will be your God.

29) I will also save you from all your uncleannesses: and I will call for the corn, and will increase it, and lay no famine upon you.

30) And I will multiply the fruit of the tree, and the increase of the field, that ye shall receive no more reproach of famine among the heathen.

DANIEL

CHAPTER 1

17) As for these four children, God gave them knowledge and skill in all learning and Wisdom: and Daniel had understanding in all visions and dreams.

CHAPTER 6

27) He delivereth and rescueth, and He worketh signs and wonders in Heaven and in earth, who hath delivered Daniel from the power of the lions.

CHAPTER 11

32) And such as do wickedly against the covenant shall be corrupt by flatteries: but the people that do know their God shall be strong, and do exploits.

CHAPTER 12

3)   And they that be wise shall shine as the brightness of the firmament; and they that turn many to righteousness as the stars for ever and ever.

HOSEA

CHAPTER 6

1)   Come, and let us return unto the Lord: for He hath torn, and He will heal us; He hath smitten, and He will bind us up.

2)   After two days will He revive us: in the third day He will raise us up, and we shall live in His sight.

3)   Then shall we know, if we follow on to know the Lord: His going forth is prepared as the morning; and He shall come unto us as the rain, as the latter and former rain unto the earth.

CHAPTER 10

12)   Sow to yourselves in righteousness, reap in mercy; break up your fallow ground: for it is time to seek the Lord, till He come and rain righteousness upon you.

CHAPTER 14

4)   I will heal their backsliding, I will love them freely: for Mine anger is turned away from him.

5)   I will be as the dew unto Israel: he shall grow as the lily, and cast forth his roots as Lebanon.

6)   His branches shall spread, and his beauty

shall be as the olive tree, and his smell as Lebanon.

7) They that dwell under his shadow shall return; they shall revive as the corn, and grow as the vine: the scent thereof shall be as the wine of Lebanon.

JOEL

CHAPTER 2

13) And rend your heart, and not your garments, and turn unto the Lord your God: for He is gracious and merciful, slow to anger, and of great kindness, and repenteth him of the evil.

19) Yea, the Lord will answer and say unto His people, Behold, I will send you corn, and wine, and oil, and ye shall be satisfied therewith: and I will no more make you a reproach among the heathen:

21) Fear not, O land; be glad and rejoice: for the Lord will do great things.

23) Be glad then, ye children of Zion, and rejoice in the Lord your God: for He hath given you the former rain moderately, and He will cause to come down for you the rain, the former rain, and the latter rain in the first month.

24) And the floors shall be full of wheat, and the vats shall overflow with wine and oil.

25) And I will restore to you the years that the locust hath eaten, the cankerworm, and the caterpiller, and the palmerworm, My great army which I sent among you.

26) And ye shall eat in plenty, and be satisfied, and praise the name of the Lord your God, that hath

dealt wondrously with you: and My people shall never be ashamed.

27) And ye shall know that I am in the midst of Israel, and that I am the Lord your God, and none else: and My people shall never be ashamed.

28) And it shall come to pass afterward, that I will pour out My Spirit upon all flesh; and your sons and your daughters shall prophesy, your old men shall dream dreams, your young men shall see visions:

29) And also upon the servants and upon the handmaids in those days will I pour out My Spirit.

30) And I will shew wonders in the Heavens and in the earth, blood, and fire, and pillars of smoke.

31) The sun shall be turned into darkness, and the moon into blood, before the great and the terrible day of the Lord come.

32) And it shall come to pass, that whosoever shall call on the name of the Lord shall be delivered: for in mount Zion and in Jerusalem shall be deliverance, as the Lord hath said, and in the remnant whom the Lord shall call.

AMOS

CHAPTER 3

7) Surely the Lord God will do nothing, but He revealeth His secret unto His servants the prophets.

CHAPTER 5

6) Seek the Lord, and ye shall live;

CHAPTER 9

13) Behold, the days come, saith the Lord, that the plowman shall overtake the reaper, and the treader of grapes him that soweth Seed; and the mountains shall drop sweet wine, and all the hills shall melt.

14) And I will bring again the captivity of my people of Israel, and they shall build the waste cities, and inhabit them; and they shall plant vineyards, and drink the wine thereof; they shall also make gardens, and eat the fruit of them.

15) And I will plant them upon their land, and they shall no more be pulled up out of their land which I have given them, saith the Lord thy God.

MICAH

CHAPTER 7

18) Who is a God like unto thee, that pardoneth iniquity, and passeth by the transgression of the remnant of His heritage? He retaineth not His anger for ever, because He delighteth in mercy.

19) He will turn again, He will have compassion upon us; He will subdue our iniquities; and Thou wilt cast all their sins into the depths of the sea.

NAHUM

CHAPTER 1

7) The Lord is good, a strong hold in the day of trouble; and He knoweth them that trust in Him.

HABAKKUK

CHAPTER 1

5)   Behold ye among the heathen, and regard, and wonder marvellously: for I will work a work in your days, which ye will not believe, though it be told you.

CHAPTER 2

3)   For the vision is yet for an appointed time, but at the end it shall speak, and not lie: though it tarry, wait for it; because it will surely come, it will not tarry.

CHAPTER 3

19) The Lord God is my strength, and He will make my feet like hinds' feet, and He will make me to walk upon mine high places. To the chief singer on my stringed instruments.

HAGGAI

CHAPTER 2

9)   The glory of this latter house shall be greater than of the former, saith the Lord of hosts: and in this place will I give peace, saith the Lord of hosts.

ZECHARIAH

CHAPTER 4

6)   Then He answered and spake unto me, saying, This is the word of the Lord unto Zerubbabel, saying, Not by might, nor by power, but by My Spirit, saith the Lord of hosts.

CHAPTER 8

12) For the Seed shall be prosperous; the vine shall give her fruit, and the ground shall give her increase, and the Heavens shall give their dew; and I will cause the remnant of this people to possess all these things.

CHAPTER 9

15) The Lord of hosts shall defend them; and they shall devour, and subdue with sling stones; and they shall drink, and make a noise as through wine; and they shall be filled like bowls, and as the corners of the altar.

16) And the Lord their God shall save them in that day as the flock of His people: for they shall be as the stones of a crown, lifted up as an ensign upon His land.

17) For how great is His goodness, and how great is His beauty! corn shall make the young men cheerful, and new wine the maids.

CHAPTER 10

1) Ask ye of the Lord rain in the time of the latter rain; so the Lord shall make bright clouds, and give them showers of rain, to every one grass in the field.

5) And they shall be as mighty men, which tread down their enemies in the mire of the streets in the battle: and they shall fight, because the Lord is with them, and the riders on horses shall be confounded.

MALACHI

CHAPTER 3

6) For I am the Lord, I change not; therefore ye sons of Jacob are not consumed.

10) Bring ye all the tithes into the storehouse, that there may be meat in mine house, and prove me now herewith, saith the Lord of hosts, if I will not open you the windows of Heaven, and pour you out a blessing, that there shall not be room enough to receive it.

11) And I will rebuke the devourer for your sakes, and he shall not destroy the fruits of your ground; neither shall your vine cast her fruit before the time in the field, saith the Lord of hosts.

12) And all nations shall call you blessed: for ye shall be a delightsome land, saith the Lord of hosts.

16) Then they that feared the Lord spake often one to another: and the Lord hearkened, and heard it, and a book of remembrance was written before Him for them that feared the Lord, and that thought upon His name.

17) And they shall be Mine, saith the Lord of hosts, in that day when I make up My jewels; and I will spare them, as a man spareth his own son that serveth him.

CHAPTER 4

2) But unto you that fear My name shall the Sun of righteousness arise with healing in His wings; and ye shall go forth, and grow up as calves of the stall.

3)   And ye shall tread down the wicked; for they shall be ashes under the soles of your feet in the day that I shall do this, saith the Lord of hosts.

THE BLESSINGS...
NEW TESTAMENT

MATTHEW

CHAPTER 2

19) But when Herod was dead, behold, an angel of the Lord appeareth in a dream to Joseph in Egypt,

20) Saying, Arise, and take the young child and His mother, and go into the land of Israel: for they are dead which sought the young child's life.

CHAPTER 4

11) Then the devil leaveth Him, and, behold, angels came and ministered unto Him.

23) And Jesus went about all Galilee, teaching in their synagogues, and preaching the gospel of the kingdom, and healing all manner of sickness and all manner of disease among the people.

24) And His fame went throughout all Syria: and they brought unto Him all sick people that were taken with divers diseases and torments, and those

which were possessed with devils, and those which were lunatic, and those that had the palsy; and He healed them.

CHAPTER 5

3)   Blessed are the poor in spirit: for theirs is the kingdom of Heaven.

4)   Blessed are they that mourn: for they shall be comforted.

5)   Blessed are the meek: for they shall inherit the earth.

6)   Blessed are they which do hunger and thirst after righteousness: for they shall be filled.

7)   Blessed are the merciful: for they shall obtain mercy.

8)   Blessed are the pure in heart: for they shall see God.

9)   Blessed are the peacemakers: for they shall be called the children of God.

10) Blessed are they which are persecuted for righteousness' sake: for theirs is the kingdom of Heaven.

11) Blessed are ye, when men shall revile you, and persecute you, and shall say all manner of evil against you falsely, for My sake.

12) Rejoice, and be exceeding glad: for great is your reward in Heaven: for so persecuted they the prophets which were before you.

CHAPTER 6

3)   But when thou doest alms, let not thy left hand know what thy right hand doeth:

4)   That thine alms may be in secret: and thy Father which seeth in secret Himself shall reward thee openly.

6)   But thou, when thou prayest, enter into thy closet, and when thou hast shut thy door, pray to thy Father which is in secret; and thy Father which seeth in secret shall reward thee openly.

8)   Be not ye therefore like unto them: for your Father knoweth what things ye have need of, before ye ask Him.

14)   For if ye forgive men their trespasses, your heavenly Father will also forgive you:

17)   But thou, when thou fastest, anoint thine head, and wash thy face;

18)   That thou appear not unto men to fast, but unto thy Father which is in secret: and thy Father, which seeth in secret, shall reward thee openly.

25)   Therefore I say unto you, Take no thought for your life, what ye shall eat, or what ye shall drink; nor yet for your body, what ye shall put on. Is not the life more than meat, and the body than raiment?

26)   Behold the fowls of the air: for they sow not, neither do they reap, nor gather into barns; yet your heavenly Father feedeth them. Are ye not much better than they?

28)   And why take ye thought for raiment? Consider the lilies of the field, how they grow; they toil not, neither do they spin:

29)   And yet I say unto you, That even Solomon in all his glory was not arrayed like one of these.

30)   Wherefore, if God so clothe the grass of the field, which to-day is, and to-morrow is cast into the oven, shall He not much more clothe you, O ye of

little faith?

31) Therefore take no thought, saying, What shall we eat? or, What shall we drink? or, Wherewithal shall we be clothed?

32) (For after all these things do the Gentiles seek:) for your heavenly Father knoweth that ye have need of all these things.

33) But seek ye first the kingdom of God, and His righteousness; and all these things shall be added unto you.

34) Take therefore no thought for the morrow: for the morrow shall take thought for the things of itself. Sufficient unto the day is the evil thereof.

CHAPTER 7

7) Ask, and it shall be given you; seek, and ye shall find; knock, and it shall be opened unto you:

8) For every one that asketh receiveth; and he that seeketh findeth; and to him that knocketh it shall be opened.

9) Or what man is there of you, whom if his son ask bread, will he give him a stone?

10) Or if he ask a fish, will he give him a serpent?

11) If ye then, being evil, know how to give good gifts unto your children, how much more shall your Father which is in Heaven give good things to them that ask Him?

24) Therefore whosoever heareth these sayings of Mine, and doeth them, I will liken him unto a wise man, which built his house upon a rock:

25) And the rain descended, and the floods came, and the winds blew, and beat upon that house; and it fell not: for it was founded upon a rock.

CHAPTER 8

16) When the even was come, they brought unto Him many that were possessed with devils: and He cast out the spirits with His word, and healed all that were sick:

17) That it might be fulfilled which was spoken by Esaias the prophet, saying, Himself took our infirmities, and bare our sicknesses.

CHAPTER 9

35) And Jesus went about all the cities and villages, teaching in their synagogues, and preaching the gospel of the kingdom, and healing every sickness and every disease among the people.

CHAPTER 10

1) And when He had called unto Him His twelve disciples, He gave them power against unclean spirits, to cast them out, and to heal all manner of sickness and all manner of disease.

8) Heal the sick, cleanse the lepers, raise the dead, cast out devils: freely ye have received, freely give.

19) But when they deliver you up, take no thought how or what ye shall speak: for it shall be given you in that same hour what ye shall speak.

20) For it is not ye that speak, but the Spirit of your Father which speaketh in you.

39) He that findeth his life shall lose it: and he that loseth his life for My sake shall find it.

40) He that receiveth you receiveth Me, and he

that receiveth Me receiveth him that sent Me.

41) He that receiveth a prophet in the name of a prophet shall receive a prophet's reward; and he that receiveth a righteous man in the name of a righteous man shall receive a righteous man's reward.

42) And whosoever shall give to drink unto one of these little ones a cup of cold water only in the name of a disciple, verily I say unto you, he shall in no wise lose his reward.

CHAPTER 11

5) The blind receive their sight, and the lame walk, the lepers are cleansed, and the deaf hear, the dead are raised up, and the poor have the gospel preached to them.

28) Come unto me, all ye that labour and are heavy laden, and I will give you rest.

29) Take My yoke upon you, and learn of Me; for I am meek and lowly in heart: and ye shall find rest unto your souls.

30) For My yoke is easy, and My burden is light.

CHAPTER 12

50) For whosoever shall do the will of My Father which is in Heaven, the same is My brother, and sister, and mother.

CHAPTER 14

14) And Jesus went forth, and saw a great multitude, and was moved with compassion toward them, and He healed their sick.

35) And when the men of that place had

knowledge of Him, they sent out into all that country round about, and brought unto Him all that were diseased;

36) And besought Him that they might only touch the hem of His garment: and as many as touched were made perfectly whole.

CHAPTER 15

30) And great multitudes came unto Him, having with them those that were lame, blind, dumb, maimed, and many others, and cast them down at Jesus' feet; and He healed them:

31) Insomuch that the multitude wondered, when they saw the dumb to speak, the maimed to be whole, the lame to walk, and the blind to see: and they glorified the God of Israel.

CHAPTER 16

18) And I say also unto thee, That thou art Peter, and upon this rock I will build my church; and the gates of hell shall not prevail against it.

19) And I will give unto thee the keys of the kingdom of Heaven: and whatsoever thou shalt bind on earth shall be bound in Heaven: and whatsoever thou shalt loose on earth shall be loosed in Heaven.

24) Then said Jesus unto His disciples, If any man will come after Me, let him deny himself, and take up his cross, and follow Me.

25) For whosoever will save his life shall lose it: and whosoever will lose his life for My sake shall find it.

27) For the Son of man shall come in the glory of His Father with His angels; and then He shall reward every man according to His works.

CHAPTER 18

10) Take heed that ye despise not one of these little ones; for I say unto you, That in Heaven their angels do always behold the face of My Father which is in Heaven.

18) Verily I say unto you, Whatsoever ye shall bind on earth shall be bound in Heaven: and whatsoever ye shall loose on earth shall be loosed in Heaven.

19) Again I say unto you, That if two of you shall agree on earth as touching any thing that they shall ask, it shall be done for them of My Father which is in Heaven.

CHAPTER 19

26) But Jesus beheld them, and said unto them, With men this is impossible; but with God all things are possible.

29) And every one that hath forsaken houses, or brethren, or sisters, or father, or mother, or wife, or children, or lands, for My name's sake, shall receive an hundredfold, and shall inherit everlasting life.

CHAPTER 20

34) So Jesus had compassion on them, and touched their eyes: and immediately their eyes received sight, and they followed Him.

CHAPTER 21

21) Jesus answered and said unto them, Verily I say unto you, If ye have faith, and doubt not, ye shall not only do this which is done to the fig tree,

but also if ye shall say unto this mountain, Be thou removed, and be thou cast into the sea; it shall be done.

22) And all things, whatsoever ye shall ask in prayer, believing, ye shall receive.

CHAPTER 23

12) And whosoever shall exalt himself shall be abased; and he that shall humble himself shall be exalted.

CHAPTER 24

13) But he that shall endure unto the end, the same shall be saved.

CHAPTER 25

34) Then shall the King say unto them on His right hand, Come, ye blessed of My Father, inherit the kingdom prepared for you from the foundation of the world:

35) For I was an hungred, and ye gave Me meat: I was thirsty, and ye gave Me drink: I was a stranger, and ye took me in:

36) Naked, and ye clothed Me: I was sick, and ye visited Me: I was in prison, and ye came unto Me.

37) Then shall the righteous answer Him, saying, Lord, when saw we Thee an hungred, and fed Thee? or thirsty, and gave Thee drink?

38) When saw we Thee a stranger, and took Thee in? or naked, and clothed Thee?

39) Or when saw we Thee sick, or in prison, and came unto Thee?

40) And the King shall answer and say unto them, Verily I say unto you, Inasmuch as ye have done it unto one of the least of these My brethren, ye have done it unto Me.

MARK

CHAPTER 1

32) And at even, when the sun did set, they brought unto Him all that were diseased, and them that were possessed with devils.

33) And all the city was gathered together at the door.

34) And He healed many that were sick of divers diseases, and cast out many devils; and suffered not the devils to speak, because they knew Him.

CHAPTER 3

14) And He ordained twelve, that they should be with Him, and that He might send them forth to preach,

15) And to have power to heal sicknesses, and to cast out devils:

35) For whosoever shall do the will of God, the same is My brother, and my sister, and mother.

CHAPTER 4

22) For there is nothing hid, which shall not be manifested; neither was any thing kept secret, but that it should come abroad.

CHAPTER 6

7)   And He called unto Him the twelve, and began to send them forth by two and two; and gave them power over unclean spirits;

12)   And they went out, and preached that men should repent.

13)   And they cast out many devils, and anointed with oil many that were sick, and healed them.

56)   And whithersoever He entered, into villages, or cities, or country, they laid the sick in the streets, and besought Him that they might touch if it were but the border of His garment: and as many as touched Him were made whole.

CHAPTER 8

34)   And when He had called the people unto Him with His disciples also, He said unto them, Whosoever will come after Me, let him deny himself, and take up his cross, and follow Me.

35)   For whosoever will save his life shall lose it; but whosoever shall lose his life for My sake and the gospel's, the same shall save it.

36)   For what shall it profit a man, if he shall gain the whole world, and lose his own soul?

CHAPTER 9

23)   Jesus said unto him, If thou canst believe, all things are possible to him that believeth.

25)   When Jesus saw that the people came running together, He rebuked the foul spirit, saying unto him, Thou dumb and deaf spirit, I charge thee, come out of him, and enter no more into him.

41)   For whosoever shall give you a cup of water

to drink in My name, because ye belong to Christ, verily I say unto you, he shall not lose his reward.

CHAPTER 10

27) With men it is impossible, but not with God: for with God all things are possible.

29) Verily I say unto you, There is no man that hath left house, or brethren, or sisters, or father, or mother, or wife, or children, or lands, for My sake, and the gospel's,

30) But he shall receive an hundredfold now in this time, houses, and brethren, and sisters, and mothers, and children, and lands, with persecutions; and in the world to come eternal life.

CHAPTER 11

23) For verily I say unto you, That whosoever shall say unto this mountain, Be thou removed, and be thou cast into the sea; and shall not doubt in his heart, but shall believe that those things which he saith shall come to pass; he shall have whatsoever he saith.

24) Therefore I say unto you, What things soever ye desire, when ye pray, believe that ye receive them, and ye shall have them.

25) And when ye stand praying, forgive, if ye have aught against any: that your Father also which is in Heaven may forgive you your trespasses.

CHAPTER 14

25) Verily I say unto you, I will drink no more of the fruit of the vine, until that day that I drink it new in the kingdom of God.

CHAPTER 16

16) He that believeth and is baptized shall be saved; but he that believeth not shall be damned.

17) And these signs shall follow them that believe; In My name shall they cast out devils; they shall speak with new tongues;

18) They shall take up serpents; and if they drink any deadly thing, it shall not hurt them; they shall lay hands on the sick, and they shall recover.

LUKE

CHAPTER 4

18) The Spirit of the Lord is upon me, because He hath anointed me to preach the gospel to the poor; He hath sent me to heal the brokenhearted, to preach deliverance to the captives, and recovering of sight to the blind, to set at liberty them that are bruised,

40) Now when the sun was setting, all they that had any sick with divers diseases brought them unto Him; and He laid His hands on every one of them, and healed them.

CHAPTER 6

20) Blessed be ye poor: for yours is the kingdom of God.

21) Blessed are ye that hunger now: for ye shall be filled. Blessed are ye that weep now: for ye shall laugh.

22) Blessed are ye, when men shall hate you,

and when they shall separate you from their company, and shall reproach you, and cast out your name as evil, for the Son of man's sake.

23) Rejoice ye in that day, and leap for joy: for, behold, your reward is great in Heaven: for in the like manner did their fathers unto the prophets.

38) Give, and it shall be given unto you; good measure, pressed down, and shaken together, and running over, shall men give into your bosom. For with the same measure that ye mete withal it shall be measured to you again.

CHAPTER 9

23) If any man will come after me, let him deny himself, and take up his cross daily, and follow Me.

24) For whosoever will save his life shall lose it: but whosoever will lose his life for My sake, the same shall save it.

25) For what is a man advantaged, if he gain the whole world, and lose himself, or be cast away?

26) For whosoever shall be ashamed of Me and of My words, of him shall the Son of man be ashamed, when He shall come in His own glory, and in His Father's, and of the holy angels.

CHAPTER 10

19) Behold, I give unto you power to tread on serpents and scorpions, and over all the power of the enemy: and nothing shall by any means hurt you.

CHAPTER 11

9)   And I say unto you, Ask, and it shall be given you; seek, and ye shall find; knock, and it shall be opened unto you.

10)   For every one that asketh receiveth; and he that seeketh findeth; and to him that knocketh it shall be opened.

11)   If a son shall ask bread of any of you that is a father, will he give him a stone? or if he ask a fish, will he for a fish give him a serpent?

12)   Or if he shall ask an egg, will he offer him a scorpion?

13)   If ye then, being evil, know how to give good gifts unto your children: how much more shall your heavenly Father give the Holy Spirit to them that ask Him?

CHAPTER 12

6)   Are not five sparrows sold for two farthings, and not one of them is forgotten before God?

7)   But even the very hairs of your head are all numbered. Fear not therefore: ye are of more value than many sparrows.

8)   Also I say unto you, Whosoever shall confess Me before men, him shall the Son of man also confess before the angels of God:

10)   And whosoever shall speak a word against the Son of man, it shall be forgiven him: but unto him that blasphemeth against the Holy Ghost it shall not be forgiven.

11)   And when they bring you unto the synagogues, and unto magistrates, and powers, take

ye no thought how or what thing ye shall answer, or what ye shall say:

12) For the Holy Ghost shall teach you in the same hour what ye ought to say.

22) And He said unto His disciples, Therefore I say unto you, Take no thought for your life, what ye shall eat; neither for the body, what ye shall put on.

23) The life is more than meat, and the body is more than raiment.

24) Consider the ravens: for they neither sow nor reap; which neither have storehouse nor barn; and God feedeth them: how much more are ye better than the fowls?

27) Consider the lilies how they grow: they toil not, they spin not; and yet I say unto you, that Solomon in all his glory was not arrayed like one of these.

28) If then God so clothe the grass, which is today in the field, and tomorrow is cast into the oven; how much more will He clothe you, O ye of little faith?

29) And seek not ye what ye shall eat, or what ye shall drink, neither be ye of doubtful mind.

30) For all these things do the nations of the world seek after: and your Father knoweth that ye have need of these things.

31) But rather seek ye the kingdom of God; and all these things shall be added unto you.

32) Fear not, little flock; for it is your Father's good pleasure to give you the kingdom.

37) Blessed are those servants, whom the lord when He cometh shall find watching: verily I say unto you, that He shall gird Himself, and make them to sit down to meat, and will come forth and serve

them.

42)   And the Lord said, Who then is that faithful and wise steward, whom his lord shall make ruler over his household, to give them their portion of meat in due season?

43)   Blessed is that servant, whom his lord when he cometh shall find so doing.

44)   Of a truth I say unto you, that He will make him ruler over all that he hath.

CHAPTER 15

10)   Likewise, I say unto you, there is joy in the presence of the angels of God over one sinner that repenteth.

11)   And he said, A certain man had two sons:

12)   And the younger of them said to his father, Father, give me the portion of goods that falleth to me. And he divided unto them his living.

13)   And not many days after the younger son gathered all together, and took his journey into a far country, and there wasted his substance with riotous living.

14)   And when he had spent all, there arose a mighty famine in that land; and he began to be in want.

15)   And he went and joined himself to a citizen of that country; and he sent him into his fields to feed swine.

16)   And he would fain have filled his belly with the husks that the swine did eat: and no man gave unto him.

17)   And when he came to himself, he said, How many hired servants of my father's have bread

enough and to spare, and I perish with hunger!

18) I will arise and go to my father, and will say unto him, Father, I have sinned against Heaven, and before thee,

19) And am no more worthy to be called thy son: make me as one of thy hired servants.

20) And he arose, and came to his father. But when he was yet a great way off, his father saw him, and had compassion, and ran, and fell on his neck, and kissed him.

21) And the son said unto him, Father, I have sinned against Heaven, and in thy sight, and am no more worthy to be called thy son.

22) But the father said to his servants, Bring forth the best robe, and put it on him; and put a ring on his hand, and shoes on his feet:

23) And bring hither the fatted calf, and kill it; and let us eat, and be merry:

24) For this my son was dead, and is alive again; he was lost, and is found. And they began to be merry.

25) Now his elder son was in the field: and as he came and drew nigh to the house, he heard music and dancing.

26) And he called one of the servants, and asked what these things meant.

27) And he said unto him, Thy brother is come; and thy father hath killed the fatted calf, because he hath received him safe and sound.

28) And he was angry, and would not go in: therefore came his father out, and intreated him.

29) And he answering said to his father, Lo, these many years do I serve thee, neither transgressed I at any time thy commandment: and yet thou never

gavest me a kid, that I might make merry with my friends:

30) But as soon as this thy son was come, which hath devoured thy living with harlots, thou hast killed for him the fatted calf.

31) And he said unto him, Son, thou art ever with me, and all that I have is thine.

32) It was meet that we should make merry, and be glad: for this thy brother was dead, and is alive again; and was lost, and is found.

CHAPTER 17

6) And the Lord said, If ye had faith as a grain of mustard Seed, ye might say unto this sycamine tree, Be thou plucked up by the root, and be thou planted in the sea; and it should obey you.

CHAPTER 18

7) And shall not God avenge His own elect, which cry day and night unto Him, though He bear long with them?

8) I tell you that He will avenge them speedily.

18) And a certain ruler asked Him, saying, Good Master, what shall I do to inherit eternal life?

27) And He said, The things which are impossible with men are possible with God.

29) And He said unto them, Verily I say unto you, There is no man that hath left house, or parents, or brethren, or wife, or children, for the kingdom of God's sake,

30) Who shall not receive manifold more in this present time, and in the world to come life

everlasting.

CHAPTER 21

12) But before all these, they shall lay their hands on you, and persecute you, delivering you up to the synagogues, and into prisons, being brought before kings and rulers for My name's sake.

13) And it shall turn to you for a testimony.

14) Settle it therefore in your hearts, not to meditate before what ye shall answer:

15) For I will give you a mouth and Wisdom, which all your adversaries shall not be able to gainsay nor resist.

16) And ye shall be betrayed both by parents, and brethren, and kinsfolks, and friends; and some of you shall they cause to be put to death.

17) And ye shall be hated of all men for My name's sake.

18) But there shall not an hair of your head perish.

28) And when these things begin to come to pass, then look up, and lift up your heads; for your redemption draweth nigh.

CHAPTER 24

45) Then opened He their understanding, that they might understand the scriptures,

JOHN

CHAPTER 1

12) But as many as received Him, to them gave He power to become the sons of God, even to them that believe on His name:

CHAPTER 3

15) That whosoever believeth in Him should not perish, but have eternal life.

16) For God so loved the world, that He gave His only begotten Son, that whosoever believeth in Him should not perish, but have everlasting life.

17) For God sent not His Son into the world to condemn the world; but that the world through Him might be saved.

21) But he that doeth truth cometh to the light, that his deeds may be made manifest, that they are wrought in God.

36) He that believeth on the Son hath everlasting life: and he that believeth not the Son shall not see life; but the wrath of God abideth on him.

CHAPTER 4

13) Jesus answered and said unto her, Whosoever drinketh of this water shall thirst again:

14) But whosoever drinketh of the water that I shall give him shall never thirst; but the water that I shall give him shall be in him a well of water springing up into everlasting life.

CHAPTER 5

21) For as the Father raiseth up the dead, and quickenth them; even so the Son quickeneth whom

He will.

22) For the Father judgeth no man, but hath committed all judgment unto the Son:

24) Verily, verily, I say unto you, He that heareth My word, and believeth on Him that sent Me, hath everlasting life, and shall not come into condemnation; but is passed from death unto life.

CHAPTER 6

32) Then Jesus said unto them, Verily, verily, I say unto you, Moses gave you not that bread from Heaven; but My Father giveth you the true bread from Heaven.

33) For the bread of God is He which cometh down from Heaven, and giveth life unto the world.

35) And Jesus said unto them, I am the bread of life: he that cometh to Me shall never hunger; and he that believeth on Me shall never thirst.

37) All that the Father giveth Me shall come to Me; and him that cometh to Me I will in no wise cast out.

38) For I came down from Heaven, not to do Mine own will, but the will of Him that sent Me.

39) And this is the Father's will which hath sent Me, that of all which He hath given Me I should lose nothing, but should raise it up again at the last day.

40) And this is the will of Him that sent Me, that every one which seeth the Son, and believeth on Him, may have everlasting life: and I will raise Him up at the last day.

47) Verily, verily, I say unto you, he that believeth on Me hath everlasting life.

48) I am that bread of life.

51) I am the living bread which came down from Heaven: if any man eat of this bread, he shall live for ever: and the bread that I will give is My flesh, which I will give for the life of the world.

54) Whoso eateth My flesh, and drinketh My blood, hath eternal life; and I will raise him up at the last day.

55) For My flesh is meat indeed, and My blood is drink indeed.

56) He that eateth My flesh, and drinketh My blood, dwelleth in Me, and I in him.

57) As the living Father hath sent Me, and I live by the Father: so he that eateth Me, even he shall live by Me.

CHAPTER 7

37) In the last day, that great day of the feast, Jesus stood and cried, saying, If any man thirst, let him come unto Me, and drink.

38) He that believeth on Me, as the Scripture hath said, out of his belly shall flow rivers of living water.

CHAPTER 8

12) Then spake Jesus again unto them, saying, I am the light of the world: he that followeth Me shall not walk in darkness, but shall have the light of life.

31) Then said Jesus to those Jews which believed on Him, If ye continue in My word, then are ye My disciples indeed;

32) And ye shall know the truth, and the truth

shall make you free.

36) If the Son therefore shall make you free, ye shall be free indeed.

CHAPTER 10

9) I am the door: by Me if any man enter in, he shall be saved, and shall go in and out, and find pasture.

10) The thief cometh not, but for to steal, and to kill, and to destroy: I am come that they might have life, and that they might have it more abundantly.

11) I am the good shepherd: the good shepherd giveth his life for the sheep.

14) I am the good shepherd, and know My sheep, and am known of Mine.

27) My sheep hear My voice, and I know them, and they follow Me:

28) And I give unto them eternal life; and they shall never perish, neither shall any man pluck them out of My hand.

29) My Father, which gave them Me, is greater than all; and no man is able to pluck them out of My Father's hand.

32) Jesus answered them, Many good works have I shewed you from my Father; for which of those works do ye stone Me?

CHAPTER 11

25) Jesus said unto her, I am the resurrection, and the life: he that believeth in Me, though he were dead, yet shall he live:

26) And whosoever liveth and believeth in Me shall never die. Believest thou this?

43) And when He thus had spoken, He cried with a loud voice, Lazarus, come forth.

CHAPTER 12

46) I am come a light into the world, that whosoever believeth on Me should not abide in darkness.

CHAPTER 13

17) If ye know these things, happy are ye if ye do them.

35   By this shall all men know that ye are My disciples, if ye have love one to another.

CHAPTER 14

1)   Let not your heart be troubled: ye believe in God, believe also in Me.

2)   In My Father's house are many mansions: if it were not so, I would have told you. I go to prepare a place for you.

3)   And if I go and prepare a place for you, I will come again, and receive you unto Myself; that where I am, there ye may be also.

4)   And whither I go ye know, and the way ye know.

6)   Jesus saith unto him, I am the way, the truth, and the life: no man cometh unto the Father, but by Me.

12) Verily, verily, I say unto you, He that believeth on Me, the works that I do shall he do also; and greater works than these shall he do; because I go unto My Father.

13) And whatsoever ye shall ask in My name,

that will I do, that the Father may be glorified in the Son.

14) If ye shall ask any thing in My name, I will do it.

15) If ye love me, keep My commandments.

16) And I will pray the Father, and He shall give you another Comforter, that He may abide with you for ever;

17) Even the Spirit of truth; whom the world cannot receive, because it seeth Him not, neither knoweth Him: but ye know Him; for He dwelleth with you, and shall be in you.

18) I will not leave you comfortless: I will come to you.

19) Yet a little while, and the world seeth Me no more; but ye see Me: because I live, ye shall live also.

20) At that day ye shall know that I am in My Father, and ye in Me, and I in you.

21) He that hath My commandments, and keepeth them, he it is that loveth Me: and he that loveth Me shall be loved of My Father, and I will love him, and will manifest Myself to him.

23) Jesus answered and said unto him, If a man love Me, he will keep My words: and My Father will love him, and We will come unto him, and make Our abode with him.

26) But the Comforter, which is the Holy Ghost, whom the Father will send in My name, He shall teach you all things, and bring all things to your remembrance, whatsoever I have said unto you.

27) Peace I leave with you, My peace I give unto you: not as the world giveth, give I unto you. Let not your heart be troubled, neither let it be afraid.

CHAPTER 15

3) Now ye are clean through the word which I have spoken unto you.

7) If ye abide in Me, and My words abide in you, ye shall ask what ye will, and it shall be done unto you.

8) Herein is My Father glorified, that ye bear much fruit; so shall ye be My disciples.

9) As the Father hath loved Me, so have I loved you: continue ye in My love.

10) If ye keep My commandments, ye shall abide in My love; even as I have kept thy Father's commandments, and abide in His love.

11) These things have I spoken unto you, that My joy might remain in you, and that your joy might be full.

12) This is My commandment, That ye love one another, as I have loved you.

13) Greater love hath no man than this, that a man lay down his life for his friends.

14) Ye are My friends, if ye do whatsoever I command you.

15) Henceforth I call you not servants; for the servant knoweth not what his lord doeth: but I have called you friends; for all things that I have heard of My Father I have made known unto you.

16) Ye have not chosen Me, but I have chosen you, and ordained you, that ye should go and bring forth fruit, and that your fruit should remain: that whatsoever ye shall ask of the Father in My name, He may give it you.

CHAPTER 16

7) Nevertheless I tell you the truth; It is expedient for you that I go away: for if I go not away, the Comforter will not come unto you; but if I depart, I will send Him unto you.

13) Howbeit when He, the Spirit of truth, is come, He will guide you into all truth: for He shall not speak of Himself; but whatsoever He shall hear, that shall He speak: and He will shew you things to come.

22) And ye now therefore have sorrow: but I will see you again, and your heart shall rejoice, and your joy no man taketh from you.

23) And in that day ye shall ask Me nothing. Verily, verily, I say unto you, Whatsoever ye shall ask the Father in My name, He will give it you.

24) Hitherto have ye asked nothing in My name: ask, and ye shall receive, that your joy may be full.

25) These things have I spoken unto you in proverbs: but the time cometh, when I shall no more speak unto you in proverbs, but I shall shew you plainly of the Father.

26) At that day ye shall ask in My name: and I say not unto you, that I will pray the Father for you:

27) For the Father Himself loveth you, because ye have loved Me, and have believed that I came out from God.

33) These things I have spoken unto you, that in Me ye might have peace. In the world ye shall have tribulation: but be of good cheer; I have overcome the world.

CHAPTER 17

1) These words spake Jesus, and lifted up His eyes to Heaven, and said, Father, the hour is come; glorify Thy Son, that Thy Son also may glorify Thee:

2) As Thou hast given Him power over all flesh, that He should give eternal life to as many as Thou hast given Him.

3) And this is life eternal, that they might know Thee the only true God, and Jesus Christ, whom Thou hast sent.

4) I have glorified Thee on the earth: I have finished the work which Thou gavest Me to do.

5) And now, O Father, glorify Thou Me with Thine own self with the glory which I had with Thee before the world was.

6) I have manifested Thy name unto the men which Thou gavest Me out of the world: Thine they were, and Thou gavest them Me; and they have kept Thy word.

7) Now they have known that all things whatsoever Thou hast given Me are of Thee.

8) For I have given unto them the words which Thou gavest Me; and they have received them, and have known surely that I came out from Thee, and they have believed that Thou didst send Me.

9) I pray for them: I pray not for the world, but for them which thou hast given Me; for they are Thine.

10) And all Mine are Thine, and Thine are Mine; and I am glorified in them.

11) And now I am no more in the world, but these are in the world, and I come to Thee. Holy Father,

keep through Thine own name those whom Thou hast given Me, that they may be one, as We are.

12) While I was with them in the world, I kept them in Thy name: those that Thou gavest Me I have kept, and none of them is lost, but the son of perdition; that the Scripture might be fulfilled.

13) And now come I to Thee; and these things I speak in the world, that they might have My joy fulfilled in themselves.

14) I have given them Thy word; and the world hath hated them, because they are not of the world, even as I am not of the world.

15) I pray not that Thou shouldest take them out of the world, but that Thou shouldest keep them from the evil.

16) They are not of the world, even as I am not of the world.

17) Sanctify them through Thy truth: Thy word is truth.

18) As Thou hast sent me into the world, even so have I also sent them into the world.

19) And for their sakes I sanctify Myself, that they also might be sanctified through the truth.

20) Neither pray I for these alone, but for them also which shall believe on Me through their word;

21) That they all may be one; as Thou, Father, art in Me, and I in Thee, that they also may be one in Us: that the world may believe that Thou hast sent Me.

22) And the glory which thou gavest Me I have given them; that they may be one, even as We are one:

23) I in them, and Thou in Me, that they may be

made perfect in one; and that the world may know that Thou hast sent Me, and hast loved them, as Thou hast loved Me.

24) Father, I will that they also, whom Thou hast given Me, be with Me where I am; that they may behold My glory, which Thou hast given Me: for Thou lovedst Me before the foundation of the world.

25) O righteous Father, the world hath not known Thee: but I have known Thee, and these have known that Thou hast sent Me.

26) And I have declared unto them Thy name, and will declare it: that the love wherewith thou hast loved Me may be in them, and I in them.

CHAPTER 20

21) Then said Jesus to them again, Peace be unto you: as My Father hath sent Me, even so send I you.

ACTS

CHAPTER 1

8) But ye shall receive power, after that the Holy Ghost is come upon you: and ye shall be witnesses unto Me both in Jerusalem, and in all Judaea, and in Samaria, and unto the uttermost part of the earth.

CHAPTER 3

19) Repent ye therefore, and be converted, that your sins may be blotted out, when the times of refreshing shall come from the presence of the Lord;

CHAPTER 10

38) How God anointed Jesus of Nazareth with the Holy Ghost and with power: Who went about doing good, and healing all that were oppressed of the devil; for God was with Him.

CHAPTER 16

31) And they said, Believe on the Lord Jesus Christ, and thou shalt be saved, and thy house.

CHAPTER 17

27) That they should seek the Lord, if haply they might feel after Him, and find Him, though He be not far from every one of us:

28) For in Him we live, and move, and have our being; as certain also of your own poets have said, For we are also His offspring.

CHAPTER 20

32) And now, brethren, I commend you to God, and to the word of His grace, which is able to build you up, and to give you an inheritance among all them which are sanctified.

35) I have shewed you all things, how that so labouring ye ought to support the weak, and to remember the words of the Lord Jesus, how He said, It is more blessed to give than to receive.

ROMANS

CHAPTER 1

16) For I am not ashamed of the gospel of Christ:

for it is the power of God unto salvation to every one that believeth; to the Jew first, and also to the Greek.

17) For therein is the righteousness of God revealed from faith to faith: as it is written, The just shall live by faith.

CHAPTER 3

24) Being justified freely by His grace through the redemption that is in Christ Jesus:

CHAPTER 4

7) Saying, Blessed are they whose iniquities are forgiven, and whose sins are covered.

8) Blessed is the man to whom the Lord will not impute sin.

CHAPTER 5

1) Therefore being justified by faith, we have peace with God through our Lord Jesus Christ:

2) By whom also we have access by faith into this grace wherein we stand, and rejoice in hope of the glory of God.

3) And not only so, but we glory in tribulations also: knowing that tribulation worketh patience;

4) And patience, experience; and experience, hope:

5) And hope maketh not ashamed; because the love of God is shed abroad in our hearts by the Holy Ghost which is given unto us.

6) For when we were yet without strength, in due time Christ died for the ungodly.

7) For scarcely for a righteous man will one die: yet peradventure for a good man some would even

dare to die.

8) But God commendeth His love toward us, in that, while we were yet sinners, Christ died for us.

9) Much more then, being now justified by His blood, we shall be saved from wrath through Him.

10) For if, when we were enemies, we were reconciled to God by the death of His Son, much more, being reconciled, we shall be saved by His life.

11) And not only so, but we also joy in God through our Lord Jesus Christ, by whom we have now received the atonement.

19) For as by one man's disobedience many were made sinners, so by the obedience of one shall many be made righteous.

20) Moreover the law entered, that the offence might abound. But where sin abounded, grace did much more abound:

CHAPTER 6

4) Therefore we are buried with Him by baptism into death: that like as Christ was raised up from the dead by the glory of the Father, even so we also should walk in newness of life.

5) For if we have been planted together in the likeness of His death, we shall be also in the likeness of His resurrection:

6) Knowing this, that our old man is crucified with Him, that the body of sin might be destroyed, that henceforth we should not serve sin.

7) For he that is dead is freed from sin.

8) Now if we be dead with Christ, we believe that we shall also live with Him:

17) But God be thanked, that ye were the

204 ■ THE BLESSING BIBLE

servants of sin, but ye have obeyed from the heart
that form of doctrine which was delivered you.

18) Being then made free from sin, ye became
the servants of righteousness.

22) But now being made free from sin, and
become servants to God, ye have your fruit unto
holiness, and the end everlasting life.

23) For the wages of sin is death; but the gift of
God is eternal life through Jesus Christ our Lord.

CHAPTER 8

1)   There is therefore now no condemnation to
them which are in Christ Jesus, who walk not after
the flesh, but after the Spirit.

2)   For the law of the Spirit of life in Christ Jesus
hath made me free from the law of sin and death.

3)   For what the law could not do, in that it was
weak through the flesh, God sending His own Son in
the likeness of sinful flesh, and for sin, condemned
sin in the flesh:

4)   That the righteousness of the law might be
fulfilled in us, who walk not after the flesh, but after
the Spirit.

5)   For they that are after the flesh do mind the
things of the flesh; but they that are after the Spirit
the things of the Spirit.

6)   For to be carnally minded is death; but to be
spiritually minded is life and peace.

7)   Because the carnal mind is enmity against
God: for it is not subject to the law of God, neither
indeed can be.

8)   So then they that are in the flesh cannot
please God.

9)   But ye are not in the flesh, but in the Spirit,

if so be that the Spirit of God dwell in you. Now if any man have not the Spirit of Christ, he is none of His.

10) And if Christ be in you, the body is dead because of sin; but the Spirit is life because of righteousness.

11) But if the Spirit of Him that raised up Jesus from the dead dwell in you, He that raised up Christ from the dead shall also quicken your mortal bodies by His Spirit that dwelleth in you.

13) For if ye live after the flesh, ye shall die: but if ye through the Spirit do mortify the deeds of the body, ye shall live.

14) For as many as are led by the Spirit of God, they are the sons of God.

15) For ye have not received the spirit of bondage again to fear; but ye have received the Spirit of adoption, whereby we cry, Abba, Father.

16) The Spirit itself beareth witness with our spirit, that we are the children of God:

17) And if children, then heirs; heirs of God, and joint-heirs with Christ; if so be that we suffer with Him, that we may be also glorified together.

18) For I reckon that the sufferings of this present time are not worthy to be compared with the glory which shall be revealed in us.

19) For the earnest expectation of the creature waiteth for the manifestation of the sons of God.

20) For the creature was made subject to vanity, not willingly, but by reason of Him who hath subjected the same in hope,

21) Because the creature itself also shall be delivered from the bondage of corruption into the glorious liberty of the children of God.

24) For we are saved by hope: but hope that is seen is not hope: for what a man seeth, why doth he yet hope for?

25) But if we hope for that we see not, then do we with patience wait for it.

26) Likewise the Spirit also helpeth our infirmities: for we know not what we should pray for as we ought: but the Spirit itself maketh intercession for us with groanings which cannot be uttered.

27) And He that searcheth the hearts knoweth what is the mind of the Spirit, because He maketh intercession for the saints according to the will of God.

28) And we know that all things work together for good to them that love God, to them who are the called according to His purpose.

29) For whom He did foreknow, He also did predestinate to be conformed to the image of His Son, that He might be the firstborn among many brethren.

30) Moreover whom He did predestinate, them He also called: and whom He called, them He also justified: and whom He justified, them He also glorified.

31) What shall we then say to these things? If God be for us, who can be against us?

32) He that spared not His own son, but delivered Him up for us all, how shall He not with Him also freely give us all things?

33) Who shall lay any thing to the charge of God's elect? It is God that justifieth.

34) Who is he that condemneth? It is Christ that died, yea rather, that is risen again, who is even at

the right hand of God, who also maketh intercession for us.

35) Who shall separate us from the love of Christ? shall tribulation, or distress, or persecution, or famine, or nakedness, or peril, or sword?

36) As it is written, For Thy sake we are killed all the day long; we are accounted as sheep for the slaughter.

37) Nay, in all these things we are more than conquerors through Him that loved us.

38) For I am persuaded, that neither death, nor life, nor angels, nor principalities, nor powers, nor things present, nor things to come,

39) Nor height, nor depth, nor any other creature, shall be able to separate us from the love of God, which is in Christ Jesus our Lord.

CHAPTER 10

8)   But what saith it? The word is nigh thee, even in thy mouth, and in thy heart: that is, the word of faith, which we preach;

9)   That if thou shalt confess with thy mouth the Lord Jesus, and shalt believe in thine heart that God hath raised Him from the dead, thou shalt be saved.

10) For with the heart man believeth unto righteousness; and with the mouth confession is made unto salvation.

11) For the Scripture saith, Whosoever believeth on Him shall not be ashamed.

13) For whosoever shall call upon the name of the Lord shall be saved.

14) How then shall they call on Him in whom they have not believed? and how shall they believe

in Him of whom they have not heard? and how shall they hear without a preacher?

15) And how shall they preach, except they be sent? as it is written, How beautiful are the feet of them that preach the gospel of peace, and bring glad tidings of good things!

17) So then faith cometh by hearing, and hearing by the word of God.

CHAPTER 11

11) I say then, Have they stumbled that they should fall? God forbid: but rather through their fall salvation is come unto the Gentiles, for to provoke them to jealousy.

33) O the depth of the riches both of the Wisdom and knowledge of God! how unsearchable are His judgments, and His ways past finding out!

CHAPTER 12

5) So we, being many, are one body in Christ, and every one members one of another.

6) Having then gifts differing according to the grace that is given to us, whether prophecy, let us prophesy according to the proportion of faith;

7) Or ministry, let us wait on our ministering: or he that teacheth, on teaching;

8) Or he that exhorteth, on exhortation: he that giveth, let him do it with simplicity; he that ruleth, with diligence; he that sheweth mercy, with cheerfulness.

14) Bless them which persecute you: bless, and curse not.

20) Therefore if thine enemy hunger, feed him; if he thirst, give him drink: for in so doing thou shalt

heap coals of fire on his head.

CHAPTER 14

17) For the kingdom of God is not meat and drink; but righteousness, and peace, and joy in the Holy Ghost.

CHAPTER 15

4) For whatsoever things were written aforetime were written for our learning, that we through patience and comfort of the Scriptures might have hope.

13) Now the God of hope fill you with all joy and peace in believing, that ye may abound in hope, through the power of the Holy Ghost.

14) And I myself also am persuaded of you, my brethren, that ye also are full of goodness, filled with all knowledge, able also to admonish one another.

CHAPTER 16

20) And the God of peace shall bruise satan under your feet shortly. The grace of our Lord Jesus Christ be with you. Amen.

1 CORINTHIANS

CHAPTER 1

9) God is faithful, by whom ye were called unto the fellowship of His Son Jesus Christ our Lord.

18) For the preaching of the cross is to them that perish foolishness; but unto us which are saved it is the power of God.

25) Because the foolishness of God is wiser than men; and the weakness of God is stronger than men.

27) But God hath chosen the foolish things of the world to confound the wise; and God hath chosen the weak things of the world to confound the things which are mighty;

28) And base things of the world, and things which are despised, hath God chosen, yea, and things which are not, to bring to nought things that are:

29) That no flesh should glory in His presence.

30) But of Him are ye in Christ Jesus, who of God is made unto us Wisdom, and righteousness, and sanctification, and redemption:

CHAPTER 2

4) And my speech and my preaching was not with enticing words of man's Wisdom, but in demonstration of the Spirit and of power:

9) But as it is written, Eye hath not seen, nor ear heard, neither have entered into the heart of man, the things which God hath prepared for them that love Him.

10) But God hath revealed them unto us by His Spirit: for the Spirit searcheth all things, yea, the deep things of God.

11) For what man knoweth the things of a man, save the spirit of man which is in him? even so the things of God knoweth no man, but the Spirit of God.

12) Now we have received, not the spirit of the world, but the Spirit which is of God; that we might know the things that are freely given to us of God.

16) For who hath known the mind of the Lord, that He may instruct him? But we have the mind of Christ.

CHAPTER 3

7)   So then neither is he that planteth any thing, neither he that watereth; but God that giveth the increase.

8)   Now he that planteth and he that watereth are one: and every man shall receive his own reward according to his own labour.

9)   For we are labourers together with God: ye are God's husbandry, ye are God's building.

CHAPTER 4

4)   For I know nothing by myself; yet am I not hereby justified: but He that judgeth me is the Lord.

CHAPTER 6

14) And God hath both raised up the Lord, and will also raise up us by His own power.

15) Know ye not that your bodies are the members of Christ? shall I then take the members of Christ, and make them the members of an harlot? God forbid.

16) What? know ye not that he which is joined to an harlot is one body? for two, saith He, shall be one flesh.

17) But he that is joined unto the Lord is one spirit.

CHAPTER 7

10) And unto the married I command, yet not I, but the Lord, Let not the wife depart from her husband:

11) But and if she depart, let her remain unmarried, or be reconciled to her husband: and let not the husband put away his wife.

12) But to the rest speak I, not the Lord: If any brother hath a wife that believeth not, and she be pleased to dwell with him, let him not put her away.

13) And the woman which hath an husband that believeth not, and if he be pleased to dwell with her, let her not leave him.

14) For the unbelieving husband is sanctified by the wife, and the unbelieving wife is sanctified by the husband: else were your children unclean; but now are they holy.

15) But if the unbelieving depart, let him depart. A brother or a sister is not under bondage in such cases: but God hath called us to peace.

16) For what knowest thou, O wife, whether thou shalt save thy husband? or how knowest thou, O man, whether thou shalt save thy wife?

17) But as God hath distributed to every man, as the Lord hath called every one, so let him walk. And so ordain I in all churches.

CHAPTER 9

24) Know ye not that they which run in a race run all, but one receiveth the prize? So run, that we may obtain.

25) And every man that striveth for the mastery is temperate in all things. Now they do it to obtain a corruptible crown; but we an incorruptible.

CHAPTER 10

13) There hath no temptation taken you but

such as is common to man: but God is faithful, who will not suffer you to be tempted above that ye are able; but will with the temptation also make a way to escape, that ye may be able to bear it.

CHAPTER 12

4) Now there are diversities of gifts, but the same Spirit.

5) And there are differences of administrations, but the same Lord.

6) And there are diversities of operations, but it is the same God which worketh all in all.

7) But the manifestation of the Spirit is given to every man to profit withal.

8) For to one is given by the Spirit the word of Wisdom; to another the word of knowledge by the same Spirit;

9) To another faith by the same Spirit; to another the gifts of healing by the same Spirit;

10) To another the working of miracles; to another prophecy; to another discerning of spirits; to another divers kinds of tongues; to another the interpretation of tongues:

11) But all these worketh that one and the selfsame Spirit, dividing to every man severally as he will.

18) But now hath God set the members every one of them in the body, as it hath pleased Him.

CHAPTER 13

8) Charity never faileth: but whether there be prophecies, they shall fail; whether there be tongues, they shall cease; whether there be knowledge, it shall vanish away.

214 ■ THE BLESSING BIBLE

12) For now we see through a glass, darkly; but then face to face: now I know in part; but then shall I know even as also I am known.

2 CORINTHIANS

CHAPTER 1

4) Who comforteth us in all our tribulation, that we may be able to comfort them which are in any trouble, by the comfort wherewith we ourselves are comforted of God.

5) For as the sufferings of Christ abound in us, so our consolation also aboundeth by Christ.

6) And whether we be afflicted, it is for your consolation and salvation, which is effectual in the enduring of the same sufferings which we also suffer: or whether we be comforted, it is for your consolation and salvation.

7) And our hope of you is stedfast, knowing, that as ye are partakers of the sufferings, so shall ye be also of the consolation.

CHAPTER 2

14) Now thanks be unto God, which always causeth us to triumph in Christ, and maketh manifest the savour of His knowledge by us in every place.

CHAPTER 3

4) And such trust have we through Christ to God-ward:

5) Not that we are sufficient of ourselves to

think any thing as of ourselves; but our sufficiency is of God;

CHAPTER 4

6)   For God, who commanded the light to shine out of darkness, hath shined in our hearts, to give the light of the knowledge of the glory of God in the face of Jesus Christ.

7)   But we have this treasure in earthen vessels, that the excellency of the power may be of God, and not of us.

8)   We are troubled on every side, yet not distressed; we are perplexed, but not in despair;

9)   Persecuted, but not forsaken; cast down, but not destroyed;

10)   Always bearing about in the body the dying of the Lord Jesus, that the life also of Jesus might be made manifest in our body.

16)   For which cause we faint not; but though our outward man perish, yet the inward man is renewed day by day.

17)   For our light affliction, which is but for a moment, worketh for us a far more exceeding and eternal weight of glory;

18)   While we look not at the things which are seen, but at the things which are not seen: for the things which are seen are temporal; but the things which are not seen are eternal.

CHAPTER 5

7)   (For we walk by faith, not by sight:)

17)   Therefore if any man be in Christ, he is a new creature: old things are passed away; behold,

all things are become new.

21) For He hath made Him to be sin for us, who knew no sin; that we might be made the righteousness of God in Him.

CHAPTER 6

16) And what agreement hath the temple of God with idols? for ye are the temple of the living God; as God hath said, I will dwell in them, and walk with them; and I will be their God, and they shall be my people.

18) And will be a Father unto you, and ye shall be my sons and daughters, saith the Lord Almighty.

CHAPTER 8

9) For ye know the grace of our Lord Jesus Christ, that, though He was rich, yet for your sakes He became poor, that ye through His poverty might be rich.

CHAPTER 9

6) But this I say, He which soweth sparingly shall reap also sparingly; and he which soweth bountifully shall reap also bountifully.

7) Every man according as he purposeth in his heart, so let him give; not grudgingly, or of necessity: for God loveth a cheerful giver.

8) And God is able to make all grace about toward you; that ye, always having all sufficiency in all things, may abound to every good work:

9) (As it is written, He hath dispersed abroad; He hath given to the poor: His righteousness

remaineth for ever.

10)   Now He that ministereth Seed to the sower both minister bread for your food, and multiply your Seed sown, and increase the fruits of your righteousness;)

11)   Being enriched in every thing to all bountifulness, which causeth through us thanksgiving to God.

12)   For the administration of this service not only supplieth the want of the saints, but is abundant also by many thanksgivings unto God;

CHAPTER 10

4)   (For the weapons of our warfare are not carnal, but mighty through God to the pulling down of strong holds;)

CHAPTER 12

9)   And He said unto me, My grace is sufficient for thee: for My strength is made perfect in weakness. Most gladly therefore will I rather glory in my infirmities, that the power of Christ may rest upon me.

GALATIANS

CHAPTER 2

20)   I am crucified with Christ: nevertheless I live; yet not I, but Christ liveth in me: and the life which I now live in the flesh I live by the faith of the Son of God, who loved me, and gave Himself for me.

CHAPTER 3

11) But that no man is justified by the law in the sight of God, it is evident: for, The just shall live by faith.

CHAPTER 5

22) But the fruit of the Spirit is love, joy, peace, longsuffering, gentleness, goodness, faith,

23) Meekness, temperance: against such there is no law.

CHAPTER 6

2) Bear ye one another's burdens, and so fulfil the law of Christ.

9) And let us not be weary in well doing: for in due season we shall reap, if we faint not.

EPHESIANS

CHAPTER 1

3) Blessed be the God and Father of our Lord Jesus Christ, who hath blessed us with all spiritual blessings in heavenly places in Christ:

4) According as He hath chosen us in Him before the foundation of the world, that we should be holy and without blame before Him in love:

5) Having predestinated us unto the adoption of children by Jesus Christ to Himself, according to the good pleasure of His will,

6) To the praise of the glory of His grace, wherein He hath made us accepted in the beloved.

7)   In Whom we have redemption through His blood, the forgiveness of sins, according to the riches of His grace;

8)   Wherein He hath abounded toward us in all Wisdom and prudence;

9)   Having made known unto us the mystery of His will, according to His good pleasure which He hath purposed in Himself;

10) That in the dispensation of the fulness of times He might gather together in one all things in Christ, both which are in Heaven, and which are on earth; even in Him:

11) In whom also we have obtained an inheritance, being predestinated according to the purpose of Him who worketh all things after the counsel of His own will:

12) That we should be to the praise of His glory, who first trusted in Christ.

18) The eyes of your understanding being enlightened; that ye may know what is the hope of His calling, and what the riches of the glory of His inheritance in the saints,

19) And what is the exceeding greatness of His power to us-ward who believe, according to the working of His mighty power,

CHAPTER 2

4)   But God, who is rich in mercy, for His great love wherewith He loved us,

5)   Even when we were dead in sins, hath quickened us together with Christ, (by grace ye are saved;)

6)   And hath raised us up together, and made

us sit together in heavenly places in Christ Jesus:

7)   That in the ages to come He might shew the exceeding riches of His grace in His kindness toward us through Christ Jesus.

8)   For by grace are ye saved through faith; and that not of yourselves: it is the gift of God:

9)   Not of works, lest any man should boast.

10) For we are His workmanship, created in Christ Jesus unto good works, which God hath before ordained that we should walk in them.

13) But now in Christ Jesus ye who sometimes were far off are made nigh by the blood of Christ.

14) For He is our peace, who hath made both one, and hath broken down the middle wall of partition between us;

19) Now therefore ye are no more strangers and foreigners, but fellow-citizens with the saints, and of the household of God;

20) And are built upon the foundation of the apostles and prophets, Jesus Christ Himself being the chief corner stone;

21) In whom all the building fitly framed together groweth unto an holy temple in the Lord:

22) In whom ye also are builded together for an habitation of God through the Spirit.

CHAPTER 3

16) That He would grant you, according to the riches of His glory, to be strengthened with might by His Spirit in the inner man;

20) Now unto Him that is able to do exceeding abundantly above all that we ask or think, according to the power that worketh in us,

21) Unto Him be glory in the church by Christ Jesus throughout all ages, world without end. Amen.

CHAPTER 6

8) Knowing that whatsoever good thing any man doeth, the same shall He receive of the Lord, whether He be bond or free.

9) And, ye masters, do the same things unto them, forebearing threatening: knowing that your Master also is in Heaven; neither is there respect of persons with him.

10) Finally, my brethren, be strong in the Lord, and in the power of His might.

11) Put on the whole armour of God, that we may be able to stand against the wiles of the devil.

12) For we wrestle not against flesh and blood, but against principalities, against powers, against the rulers of the darkness of this world, against spiritual wickedness in high places.

13) Wherefore take unto you the whole armour of God, that ye may be able to withstand in the evil day, and having done all, to stand.

14) Stand therefore, having your loins girt about with truth, and having on the breastplate of righteousness;

15) And your feet shod with the preparation of the gospel of peace;

16) Above all, taking the shield of faith, wherewith ye shall be able to quench all the fiery darts of the wicked.

17) And take the helmet of salvation, and the sword of the Spirit, which is the word of God:

PHILIPPIANS

CHAPTER 1

6) Being confident of this very thing, that He which hath begun a good work in you will perform [it] until the day of Jesus Christ:

CHAPTER 2

13) For it is God which worketh in you both to will and to do of His good pleasure.

CHAPTER 4

6) Be careful for nothing; but in every thing by prayer and supplication with thanksgiving let your requests be made known unto God.

7) And the peace of God, which passeth all understanding, shall keep your hearts and minds through Christ Jesus.

8) Finally, brethren, whatsoever things are true, whatsoever things are honest, whatsoever things are just, whatsoever things are pure, whatsoever things are lovely, whatsoever things are of good report; if there be any virtue, and if there be any praise, think on these things.

13) I can do all things through Christ which strengthened me.

19) But my God shall supply all your need according to His riches in glory by Christ Jesus.

COLOSSIANS

CHAPTER 1

10) That ye might walk worthy of the Lord unto all pleasing, being fruitful in every good work, and increasing in the knowledge of God;

11) Strengthened with all might, according to His glorious power, unto all patience and longsuffering with joyfulness;

12) Giving thanks unto the Father, which hath made us meet to be partakers of the inheritance of the saints in light:

13) Who hath delivered us from the power of darkness, and hath translated us into the kingdom of His dear Son:

14) In Whom we have redemption through His blood, even the forgiveness of sins:

CHAPTER 3

23) And whatsoever ye do, do it heartily, as to the Lord, and not unto men;

24) Knowing that of the Lord ye shall receive the reward of the inheritance: for ye serve the Lord Christ.

1 THESSALONIANS

CHAPTER 5

9) For God hath not appointed us to wrath, but to obtain salvation by our Lord Jesus Christ,

23) And the very God of peace sanctify you wholly; and I pray God your whole spirit and soul and body be preserved blameless unto the coming of our Lord Jesus Christ.

2 THESSALONIANS

CHAPTER 3

2)   And that we may be delivered from unreasonable and wicked men: for all men have not faith.

3)   But the Lord is faithful, who shall stablish you, and keep you from evil.

5)   And the Lord direct your hearts into the love of God, and into the patient waiting for Christ.

16) Now the Lord of peace Himself give you peace always by all means. The Lord be with you all.

1 TIMOTHY

CHAPTER 1

14) And the grace of our Lord was exceeding abundant with faith and love which is in Christ Jesus.

15) This is a faithful saying, and worthy of all acceptation, that Christ Jesus came into the world to save sinners; of whom I am chief.

2 TIMOTHY

CHAPTER 1

7)   For God hath not given us the spirit of fear; but of power, and of love, and of a sound mind.

12) For the which cause I also suffer these

things: nevertheless I am not ashamed: for I know whom I have believed, and am persuaded that He is able to keep that which I have committed unto Him against that day.

CHAPTER 2

7) Consider what I say; and the Lord give thee understanding in all things.

11) It is a faithful saying: For if we be dead with Him, we shall also live with Him:

12) If we suffer, we shall also reign with Him: if we deny Him, He also will deny us:

13) If we believe not, yet He abideth faithful: He cannot deny Himself.

CHAPTER 4

18) And the Lord shall deliver me from every evil work, and will preserve me unto His heavenly kingdom: to Whom be glory for ever and ever. Amen.

TITUS

CHAPTER 1

2) In hope of eternal life, which God, that cannot lie, promised before the world began;

CHAPTER 3

5) Not by works of righteousness which we have done, but according to His mercy He saved us, by the washing of regeneration, and renewing of the Holy Ghost;

6) Which He shed on us abundantly through Jesus Christ our Saviour;

7) That being justified by His grace, we should be made heirs according to the hope of eternal life.

HEBREWS

CHAPTER 2

6) But one in a certain place testified, saying, What is man, that thou art mindful of Him? or the Son of man, that thou visitest Him?

7) Thou madest Him a little lower than the angels; thou crownedst Him with glory and honour, and didst set Him over the works of thy hands:

8) Thou hast put all things in subjection under His feet. For in that He put all in subjection under Him, He left nothing that is not put under Him. But now we see not yet all things put under Him.

CHAPTER 4

14) Seeing then that we have a great high priest, that is passed into the Heavens, Jesus the Son of God, let us hold fast our profession.

15) For we have not an high priest which cannot be touched with the feeling of our infirmities; but was in all points tempted like as we are, yet without sin.

16) Let us therefore come boldly unto the throne of grace, that we may obtain mercy, and find grace to help in time of need.

CHAPTER 6

10) For God is not unrighteous to forget your work and labour of love, which ye have shewed

toward His name, in that ye have ministered to the saints, and do minister.

11)   And we desire that every one of you do shew the same diligence to the full assurance of hope unto the end:

12)   That ye be not slothful, but followers of them who through faith and patience inherit the promises.

13)   For when God made promise to Abraham, because He could swear by no greater, He sware by Himself,

14)   Saying, Surely blessing I will bless thee, and multiplying I will multiply thee.

15)   And so, after he had patiently endured, he obtained the promise.

17)   Wherein God, willing more abundantly to shew unto the heirs of promise the immutability of His counsel, confirmed it by an oath:

18)   That by two immutable things, in which it was impossible for God to lie, we might have a strong consolation, who have fled for refuge to lay hold upon the hope set before us:

19)   Which hope we have as an anchor of the soul, both sure and stedfast, and which entereth into that within the veil;

20)   Whither the forerunner is for us entered, even Jesus, made an high priest for ever after the order of Melchisedec.

CHAPTER 8

10)   For this is the covenant that I will make with the house of Israel after those days, saith the Lord; I will put My laws into their mind, and write them in their hearts: and I will be to them a God, and they

shall be to Me a people:

12) For I will be merciful to their unrighteousness, and their sins and their iniquities will I remember no more.

CHAPTER 9

28) So Christ was once offered to bear the sins of many; and unto them that look for Him shall He appear the second time without sin unto salvation.

CHAPTER 10

16) This is the covenant that I will make with them after those days, saith the Lord, I will put My laws into their hearts, and in their minds will I write them;

17) And their sins and iniquities will I remember no more.

18) Now where remission of these is, there is no more offering for sin.

19) Having therefore, brethren, boldness to enter into the holiest by the blood of Jesus,

20) By a new and living way, which He hath consecrated for us, through the veil, that is to say, His flesh;

21) And having an high priest over the house of God;

22) Let us draw near with a true heart in full assurance of faith, having our hearts sprinkled from an evil conscience, and our bodies washed with pure water.

23) Let us hold fast the profession of our faith without wavering; (for He is faithful that promised;)

32) But call to remembrance the former days, in which, after ye were illuminated, ye endured a great fight of afflictions;

35) Cast not away therefore your confidence, which hath great recompense of reward.

36) For ye have need of patience, that, after ye have done the will of God, ye might receive the promise.

37) For yet a little while, and he that shall come will come, and will not tarry.

38) Now the just shall live by faith: but if any man draw back, my soul shall have no pleasure in Him.

39) But we are not of them who draw back unto perdition; but of them that believe to the saving of the soul.

CHAPTER 11

1) Now faith is the substance of things hoped for, the evidence of things not seen.

2) For by it the elders obtained a good report.

3) Through faith we understand that the worlds were framed by the word of God, so that things which are seen were not made of things which do appear.

4) By faith Abel offered unto God a more excellent sacrifice than Cain, by which he obtained witness that he was righteous, God testifying of his gifts: and by it he being dead yet speaketh.

5) By faith Enoch was translated that he should not see death; and was not found, because God had translated him: for before his translation he had this testimony, that he pleased God.

6) But without faith it is impossible to please Him; for he that cometh to God must believe that He is, and that He is a rewarder of them that diligently seek Him.

7) By faith Noah, being warned of God of things not seen as yet, moved with fear, prepared an ark to the saving of his house; by the which he condemned the world, and became heir of the righteousness which is by faith.

8) By faith Abraham, when he was called to go out into a place which he should after receive for an inheritance, obeyed; and he went out, not knowing whither he went.

9) By faith he sojourned in the land of promise, as in a strange country, dwelling in tabernacles with Isaac and Jacob, the heirs with him of the same promise:

10) For he looked for a city which hath foundations, whose builder and maker is God.

11) Through faith also Sara herself received strength to conceive Seed, and was delivered of a child when she was past age, because she judged Him faithful who had promised.

12) Therefore sprang there even of one, and him as good as dead, so many as the stars of the sky in multitude, and as the sand which is by the sea shore innumerable.

13) These all died in faith, not having received the promises, but having seen them afar off, and were persuaded of them, and embraced them, and confessed that they were strangers and pilgrims on the earth.

CHAPTER 12

7)   If ye endure chastening, God dealeth with you as with sons; for what son is he whom the father chasteneth not?

11)   Now no chastening for the present seemeth to be joyous, but grievous: nevertheless afterward it yieldeth the peaceable fruit of righteousness unto them which are exercised thereby.

CHAPTER 13

4)   Marriage is honourable in all, and the bed undefiled: but whoremongers and adulterers God will judge.

5)   I will never leave thee, nor forsake thee.

6)   So that we may boldly say, The Lord is my helper, and I will not fear what man shall do unto me.

8)   Jesus Christ the same yesterday, and to day, and for ever.

20)   Now the God of peace, that brought again from the dead our Lord Jesus, that great shepherd of the sheep, through the blood of the everlasting covenant,

21)   Make you perfect in every good work to do His will, working in you that which is well pleasing in His sight, through Jesus Christ; to Whom be glory for ever and ever. Amen.

JAMES

CHAPTER 1

2)   My brethren, count it all joy when ye fall into divers temptations;

3)   Knowing this, that the trying of your faith worketh patience.

4)   But let patience have her perfect work, that ye may be perfect and entire, wanting nothing.

5)   If any of you lack Wisdom, let him ask of God, that giveth to all men liberally, and upbraideth not; and it shall be given him.

6)   But let him ask in faith, nothing wavering. For he that wavereth is like a wave of the sea driven with the wind and tossed.

12) Blessed is the man that endureth temptation: for when he is tried, he shall receive the crown of life, which the Lord hath promised to them that love Him.

17)   Every good gift and every perfect gift is from above, and cometh down from the Father of lights, with Whom is no variableness, neither shadow of turning.

25)   But whoso looketh into the perfect law of liberty, and continueth therein, he being not a forgetful hearer, but a doer of the work, this man shall be blessed in his deed.

CHAPTER 3

17)   But the Wisdom that is from above is first pure, then peaceable, gentle, and easy to be entreated, full of mercy and good fruits, without partiality, and without hypocrisy.

18)   And the fruit of righteousness is sown in peace of them that make peace.

CHAPTER 4

6)   But He giveth more grace. Wherefore He saith, God resisteth the proud, but giveth grace unto the humble.

8)   Draw nigh to God, and He will draw nigh to you. Cleanse your hands, ye sinners; and purify your hearts, ye double minded.

10) Humble yourselves in the sight of the Lord, and He shall lift you up.

CHAPTER 5

11) Behold, we count them happy which endure. Ye have heard of the patience of Job, and have seen the end of the Lord; that the Lord is very pitiful, and of tender mercy.

13) Is any among you afflicted? let him pray. Is any merry? let him sing psalms.

14) Is any sick among you? let him call for the elders of the church; and let them pray over him, anointing him with oil in the name of the Lord:

15) And the prayer of faith shall save the sick, and the Lord shall raise him up; and if he have committed sins, they shall be forgiven him.

16) Confess your faults one to another, and pray one for another, that ye may be healed. The effectual fervent prayer of a righteous man availeth much.

17) Elias was a man subject to like passions as we are, and he prayed earnestly that it might not rain: and it rained not on the earth by the space of three years and six months.

18) And he prayed again, and the Heaven gave rain, and the earth brought forth her fruit.

1 PETER

CHAPTER 1

3)   Blessed be the God and Father of our Lord Jesus Christ, which according to His abundant mercy hath begotten us again unto a lively hope by the resurrection of Jesus Christ from the dead,

4)   To an inheritance incorruptible, and undefiled, and that fadeth not away, reserved in Heaven for you,

5)   Who are kept by the power of God through faith unto salvation ready to be revealed in the last time.

6)   Wherein ye greatly rejoice, though now for a season, if need be, ye are in heaviness through manifold temptations:

7)   That the trial of your faith, being much more precious than of gold that perisheth, though it be tried with fire, might be found unto praise and honour and glory at the appearing of Jesus Christ:

18)   Forasmuch as ye know that ye were not redeemed with corruptible things, as silver and gold, from your vain conversation received by tradition from your fathers;

19)   But with the precious blood of Christ, as of a lamb without blemish and without spot:

22)   Seeing ye have purified your souls in obeying the truth through the Spirit unto unfeigned love of the brethren, see that ye love one another with a pure heart fervently:

23)   Being born again, not of corruptible Seed, but of incorruptible, by the word of God, which liveth and abideth for ever.

25) But the word of the Lord endureth for ever. And this is the word which by the gospel is preached unto you.

CHAPTER 2

5) Ye also, as lively stones, are built up a spiritual house, an holy priesthood, to offer up spiritual sacrifices, acceptable to God by Jesus Christ.

9) But ye are a chosen generation, a royal priesthood, an holy nation, a peculiar people; that ye should shew forth the praises of Him who hath called you out of darkness into His marvellous light:

24) Who His own self bare our sins in His own body on the tree, that we, being dead to sins, should live unto righteousness: by Whose stripes ye were healed.

CHAPTER 3

12) For the eyes of the Lord are over the righteous, and His ears are open unto their prayers: but the face of the Lord is against them that do evil.

13) And who is he that will harm you, if ye be followers of that which is good?

14) But and if ye suffer for righteousness' sake, happy are ye: and be not afraid of their terror, neither be troubled;

17) For it is better, if the will of God be so, that ye suffer for well doing, than for evil doing.

CHAPTER 4

12) Beloved, think it not strange concerning the

fiery trial which is to try you, as through some strange thing happened unto you:

13) But rejoice, inasmuch as ye are partakers of Christ's sufferings; that, when His glory shall be revealed, ye may be glad also with exceeding joy.

14) If ye be reproached for the name of Christ, happy are ye; for the Spirit of glory and of God resteth upon you: on their part He is evil spoken of, but on your part He is glorified.

CHAPTER 5

6) Humble yourselves therefore under the mighty hand of God that He may exalt you in due time:

7) Casting all your care upon Him; for He careth for you.

10) But the God of all grace, who hath called us unto His eternal glory by Christ Jesus, after that ye have suffered a while, make you perfect, stablish, strengthen, settle you.

2 PETER

CHAPTER 1

3) According as His divine power hath given unto us all things that pertain unto life and godliness, through the knowledge of Him that hath called us to glory and virtue:

4) Whereby are given unto us exceeding great and precious promises: that by these ye might be partakers of the divine nature, having escaped the corruption that is in the world through lust.

5) And beside this, giving all diligence, add to your faith virtue; and to virtue knowledge;

6) And to knowledge temperance; and to temperance patience; and to patience godliness;

8) For if these things be in you, and abound, they make you that ye shall neither be barren nor unfruitful in the knowledge of our Lord Jesus Christ.

CHAPTER 2

9) The Lord knoweth how to deliver the godly out of temptations, and to reserve the unjust unto the day of judgment to be punished:

CHAPTER 3

9) The Lord is not slack concerning His promise, as some men count slackness; but is longsuffering to us-ward, not willing that any should perish, but that all should come to repentance.

1 JOHN

CHAPTER 1

7) But if we walk in the light, as He is in the light, we have fellowship one with another, and the blood of Jesus Christ His Son cleanseth us from all sin.

9) If we confess our sins, He is faithful and just to forgive us our sins, and to cleanse us from all unrighteousness.

CHAPTER 2

1) My little children, these things write I unto

you, that ye sin not. And if any man sin, we have an advocate with the Father, Jesus Christ the righteous:

3)   And hereby we do know that we know Him, if we keep His commandments.

5)   But whoso keepeth His word, in him verily is the love of God perfected: hereby know we that we are in Him.

8)   Again, a new commandment I write unto you, which thing is true in Him and in you: because the darkness is past, and the true light now shineth.

10) He that loveth his brother abideth in the light, and there is none occasion of stumbling in Him.

14) I have written unto you, fathers, because ye have known Him that is from the beginning. I have written unto you, young men, because ye are strong, and the word of God abideth in you, and ye have overcome the wicked one.

17) And the world passeth away, and the lust thereof: but he that doeth the will of God abideth for ever.

20) But ye have an unction from the Holy One, and ye know all things.

24) Let that therefore abide in you, which ye have heard from the beginning. If that which ye have heard from the beginning shall remain in you, ye also shall continue in the Son, and in the Father.

25) And this is the promise that He hath promised us, even eternal life.

26) These things have I written unto you concerning them that seduce you.

27) But the anointing which ye have received of

Him abideth in you, and ye need not that any man teach you: but as the same anointing teacheth you of all things, and is truth, and is no lie, and even as it hath taught you, ye shall abide in Him.

28) And now, little children, abide in Him; that, when He shall appear, we may have confidence, and not be ashamed before Him at His coming.

29) If ye know that He is righteous, ye know that every one that doeth righteousness is born of Him.

CHAPTER 3

1) Behold, what manner of love the Father hath bestowed upon us, that we should be called the sons of God: therefore the world knoweth us not, because it knew Him not.

2) Beloved, now are we the sons of God, and it doth not yet appear what we shall be: but we know that, when He shall appear, we shall be like Him; for we shall see Him as He is.

3) And every man that hath this hope in Him purifieth himself, even as He is pure.

9) Whosoever is born of God doth not commit sin; for His Seed remaineth in him; and he cannot sin, because he is born of God.

14) We know that we have passed from death unto life, because we love the brethren. He that loveth not his brother abideth in death.

16) Hereby perceive we the love of God, because He laid down his life for us: and we ought to lay down our lives for the brethren.

22) And whatsoever we ask, we receive of Him, because we keep His commandments, and do those

things that are pleasing in His sight.

23) And this is His commandment, That we should believe on the name of His Son Jesus Christ, and love one another, as He gave us commandment.

24) And he that keepeth His commandments dwelleth in Him, and He in him. And hereby we know that He abideth in us, by the Spirit which He hath given us.

CHAPTER 4

4) Ye are of God, little children, and have overcome them: because greater is He that is in you, than He that is in the world.

9) In this was manifested the love of God toward us, because that God sent His only begotten Son into the world, that we might live through Him.

10) Herein is love, not that we loved God, but that he loved us, and sent His Son to be the propitiation for our sins.

13) Hereby know we that we dwell in Him, and He in us, because He hath given us of His Spirit.

15) Whosoever shall confess that Jesus is the Son of God, God dwelleth in him, and he in God.

16) And we have known and believed the love that God hath to us. God is love; and he that dwelleth in love dwelleth in God, and God in him.

18) There is no fear in love; but perfect love casteth out fear: because fear hath torment. He that feareth is not made perfect in love.

CHAPTER 5

4) For whatsoever is born of God overcometh

the world: and this is the victory that overcometh the world, even our faith.

5) Who is he that overcometh the world, but he that believeth that Jesus is the Son of God?

11) And this is the record, that God hath given to us eternal life, and this life is in His Son.

12) He that hath the Son hath life; and he that hath not the Son of God hath not life.

13) These things have I written unto you that believe on the name of the Son of God; that ye may know that ye have eternal life, and that ye may believe on the name of the Son of God.

14) And this is the confidence that we have in Him, that, if we ask any thing according to His will, He heareth us:

15) And if we know that He hear us, whatsoever we ask, we know that we have the petitions that we desired of Him.

20) And we know that the Son of God is come, and hath given us an understanding, that we may know Him that is true, and we are in Him that is true, even in His Son Jesus Christ. This is the true God, and eternal life.

2 JOHN

CHAPTER 1

2) For the truth's sake, which dwelleth in us, and shall be with us for ever.

3 JOHN

CHAPTER 1

2)   Beloved, I wish above all things that thou mayest prosper and be in health, even as thy soul prospereth.

JUDE

CHAPTER 1

20) But ye, beloved, building up yourselves on your most holy faith, praying in the Holy Ghost,

24) Now unto Him that is able to keep you from falling, and to present you faultless before the presence of His glory with exceeding joy,

REVELATION

CHAPTER 1

7)   Behold, He cometh with clouds; and every eye shall see Him, and they also which pierced Him: and all kindreds of the earth shall wail because of Him. Even so, Amen.

17) And when I saw Him, I fell at His feet as dead. And He laid His right hand upon me, saying unto me, Fear not. I am the first and the last:

18) I am He that liveth, and was dead; and, behold, I am alive for evermore, Amen; and have the keys of hell and of death.

CHAPTER 2

7)   He that hath an ear, let him hear what the Spirit saith unto the churches; To him that overcometh will I give to eat of the tree of life, which

is in the midst of the paradise of God.

9)   I know thy works, and tribulation, and poverty, (but thou art rich) and I know the blasphemy of them which say they are Jews, and are not, but are the synagogue of Satan.

10)   Fear none of those things which thou shalt suffer: behold, the devil shall cast some of you into prison, that ye may be tried; and ye shall have tribulation ten days: be thou faithful unto death, and I will give thee a crown of life.

17)   He that hath an ear, let him hear what the Spirit saith unto the churches; To him that overcometh will I give to eat of the hidden manna, and will give him a white stone, and in the stone a new name written, which no man knoweth saving he that receiveth it.

26)   And he that overcometh, and keepeth my works unto the end, to him will I give power over the nations:

CHAPTER 3

5)   He that overcometh, the same shall be clothed in white raiment; and I will not blot out his name out of the book of life, but I will confess his name before My Father, and before His angels.

8)   I know thy works: behold, I have set before thee an open door, and no man can shut it: for thou hast a little strength, and hast kept My word, and hast not denied My name.

10) Because thou hast kept the word of My patience, I also will keep thee from the hour of temptation, which shall come upon all the world, to try them that dwell upon the earth.

12) Him that overcometh will I make a pillar in the temple of My God, and he shall go no more out: and I will write upon him the name of My God, and the name of the city of my God, which is new Jerusalem, which cometh down out of Heaven from My God: and I will write upon him My new name.

20) Behold, I stand at the door, and knock: if any man hear My voice, and open the door, I will come in to him, and will sup with him, and he with Me.

21) To him that overcometh will I grant to set with Me in My throne, even as I also overcame, and am set down with My Father in His throne.

CHAPTER 7

14) And I said unto Him, Sir, thou knowest. And He said to me, These are they which came out of great tribulation, and have washed their robes, and made them white in the blood of the Lamb.

15) Therefore are they before the throne of God, and serve Him day and night in His temple: and He that siteth on the throne shall dwell among them.

16) They shall hunger no more, neither thirst any more; neither shall the sun light on them, nor any heat.

17) For the Lamb which is in the midst of the throne shall feed them, and shall lead them unto living fountains of waters: and God shall wipe away all tears from their eyes.

CHAPTER 12

11) And they overcame him by the blood of the Lamb, and by the word of their testimony; and they loved not their lives unto the death.

CHAPTER 16

15)   Behold, I come as a thief. Blessed is he that watcheth, and keepeth his garments, lest he walk naked, and they see his shame.

CHAPTER 20

1)   And I saw an angel come down from Heaven, having the key of the bottomless pit and a great chain in his hand.

2)   And he laid hold on the dragon, that old serpent, which is the devil, and satan, and bound him a thousand years,

3)   And cast him into the bottomless pit, and shut him up, and set a seal upon him, that he should deceive the nations no more, till the thousand years should be fulfilled: and after that he must be loosed a little season.

4)   And I saw thrones, and they sat upon them, and judgment was given unto them: and I saw the souls of them that were beheaded for the witness of Jesus, and for the word of God, and which had not worshipped the beast, neither his image, neither had received his mark upon their foreheads, or in their hands; and they lived and reigned with Christ a thousand years.

6)   Blessed and holy is he that hath part in the first resurrection: on such the second death hath no power, but they shall be priests of God and of Christ, and shall reign with Him a thousand years.

CHAPTER 21

1)   And I saw a new Heaven and a new earth: for the first Heaven and the first earth were passed away; and there was no more sea.

2)   And I John saw the holy city, new Jerusalem, coming down from God out of Heaven, prepared as a bride adorned for her husband.

3)   And I heard a great voice out of Heaven saying, Behold, the tabernacle of God is with men, and He will dwell with them, and they shall be His people, and God Himself shall be with them, and be their God.

4)   And God shall wipe away all tears from their eyes; and there shall be no more death, neither sorrow, nor crying, neither shall there be any more pain: for the former things are passed away.

5)   And He that sat upon the throne said, Behold, I make all things new. And He said unto me, Write: for these words are true and faithful.

6)   And He said unto me, It is done. I am Alpha and Omega, the beginning and the end. I will give unto him that is athirst of the fountain of the water of life freely.

7)   He that overcometh shall inherit all things; and I will be his God, and he shall be My son.

CHAPTER 22

1)   And He shewed me a pure river of water of life, clear as crystal, proceeding out of the throne of God and of the Lamb.

2)   In the midst of the street of it, and on either side of the river, was there the tree of life, which bare twelve manner of fruits, and yielded her fruit every month: and the leaves of the tree were for the healing

of the nations.

3) And there shall be no more curse: but the throne of God and of the Lamb shall be in it; and His servants shall serve Him:

4) And they shall see His face; and His name shall be in their foreheads.

5) And there shall be no night there; and they need no candle, neither light of the sun; for the Lord God giveth them light; and they shall reign for ever and ever.

7) Behold, I come quickly: blessed is he that keepeth the sayings of the prophecy of this book.

12) And, behold, I come quickly; and My reward is with Me, to give every man according as his work shall be.

14) Blessed are they that do His commandments, that they may have right to the tree of life, and may enter in through the gates into the city.

17) And the Spirit and the bride say, Come. And let him that heareth say, Come. And let him that is athirst come. And whosoever will, let him take the water of life freely.

BLESSING PAGE INDEX

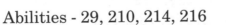

38. Ministry - 150, 198, 209, 236
39. Peace - 30, 77, 92, 135, 147, 224, 226
40. Power - 27, 33, 42, 84, 149, 176, 196, 202
41. Promotion - 32, 46, 50, 92, 172, 179, 221,
          234, 237
42. Prosperity - 21, 30, 31, 61, 80, 243
43. Protection - 22, 32, 61, 77, 95, 141, 167, 186
44. Provision - 39, 45, 56, 81, 90, 117
45. Rest - 69, 75, 119, 121, 134, 156, 177
46. Restoration - 13, 67, 74, 75, 83, 99, 114, 217
47. Resurrection - 135, 192, 195, 206, 207
48. Riches - 40, 58, 123, 129, 131, 142, 219
49. Salvation - 76, 85, 193, 203, 204, 223
50. Security - 76, 86, 87, 100, 155, 175
51. Strength - 49, 57, 72, 110, 139
52. Success - 48, 149, 224
53. Truth - 181, 194, 196, 201, 243
54. Understanding - 53, 105, 108, 119, 191, 221,
          226
55. Victory - 87, 104, 223, 242
56. Wisdom - 54, 119, 190, 233
57. Word of God - 73, 103, 107, 147, 154
58. Work - 43, 45, 68, 131

DECISION

DR. MIKE MURDOCK

Will You Accept Jesus As Your Personal Savior Today?

The Bible says, "That if thou shalt confess with thy mouth the Lord Jesus, and shalt believe in thine heart that God hath raised Him from the dead, thou shalt be saved" (Rom. 10:9).

Pray this prayer from your heart today!

"Dear Jesus, I believe that You died for me and rose again on the third day. I confess I am a sinner...I need Your love and forgiveness... Come into my heart. Forgive my sins. I receive your eternal life. Confirm Your love by giving me peace, joy and supernatural love for others. Amen."

is in tremendous demand as one of the most dynamic speakers in America today.

More than 14,000 audiences in 38 countries have attended his meetings and seminars. Hundreds of invitations come to him from churches, colleges and business corporations. He is a noted author of over 120 books, including the best sellers, *"The Leadership Secrets of Jesus"* and *"Secrets of the Richest Man Who Ever Lived."* Thousands view his weekly television program, *"Wisdom Keys with Mike Murdock."* Many attend his Saturday School of Wisdom Breakfasts that he hosts in major cities of America.

Clip and Mail

☐ Yes, Mike! I made a decision to accept Christ as my personal Savior today. Please send me my free gift of your book, *"31 Keys to a New Beginning"* to help me with my new life in Christ. *(B-48)*

NAME _____ BIRTHDAY _____

ADDRESS _____

CITY _____ STATE _____ ZIP _____

PHONE _____ E-MAIL _____ *B-28*

Mail form to:
The Wisdom Center • *P. O. Box 99* •*Denton, TX 76202*
Phone: 1-888-WISDOM-1 (1-888-947-3661)
Website: ***www.thewisdomcenter.cc***

251

THE MAN
DR. MIKE MURDOCK

1 Has embraced his Assignment to Pursue...Proclaim...and Publish the Wisdom of God to help people achieve their dreams and goals.

2 Began full-time evangelism at the age of 19, which has continued since 1966.

3 Has traveled and spoken to more than 14,000 audiences in 38 countries, including East and West Africa, the Orient, and Europe.

4 Noted author of 120 books, including best sellers, "Wisdom For Winning," "Dream Seeds" and "The Double Diamond Principle."

5 Created the popular "Topical Bible" series for Businessmen, Mothers, Fathers, Teenagers; "The One-Minute Pocket Bible" series, and "The Uncommon Life" series.

6 Has composed more than 5,700 songs such as "I Am Blessed," "You Can Make It," "God Rides On Wings Of Love" and "Jesus Just The Mention Of Your Name," recorded by many gospel artists.

7 Is the Founder of The Wisdom Center, in Denton, Texas.

8 Has a weekly television program called "Wisdom Keys With Mike Murdock."

9 Has appeared often on TBN, CBN and other television network programs.

10 Is a Founding Trustee on the Board of International Charismatic Bible Ministries with Oral Roberts.

11 Has had more than 3,500 accept the call into full-time ministry under his ministry.

THE
MINISTRY

1 Wisdom Books & Literature Over 120 best-selling Wisdom Books and 70 Teaching Tape Series.

2 Church Crusades - Multitudes are ministered to in crusades and seminars throughout America in "The Mike Murdock School Of Wisdom." Known as a man who loves pastors has focused on church crusades for 36 years.

3 Music Ministry - Millions have been blessed by the anointed songwriting and singing of Mike Murdock, who has made over 15 music albums and CDs available.

4 Television - "Wisdom Keys With Mike Murdock," a nationally-syndicated weekly television program.

5 The Wisdom Center - The Ministry Offices where Dr. Murdock holds an annual School of Wisdom for those desiring The Uncommon Life.

6 Schools of the Holy Spirit - Mike Murdock hosts Schools of the Holy Spirit in many churches to mentor believers on the Person and companionship of the Holy Spirit.

7 Schools of Wisdom - In 24 major cities Mike Murdock hosts Saturday Schools of Wisdom for those who want personalized and advanced training for achieving "The Uncommon Life."

8 Missionary Ministry - Dr. Murdock's overseas outreaches to 38 countries have included crusades in East and West Africa, South America and Europe.

Your Letter Is Very Important to Me

You are a special person to me, and I believe that you are special to God. I want to assist you in any way possible. Write me when you need an intercessor to pray for you. When you write, my staff and I will pray over your letter. I will write you back.

Mike, please enter into the prayer of agreement with me for the following needs:
(Please Print)

_____

_____

_____

_____

_____

_____

_____

_____

_____

_____

_____

_____

_____

Mail to:
The Wisdom Center • *P. O. Box 99* •*Denton, TX 76202*
Phone: 1-888-WISDOM-1 (1-888-947-3661)
Website: ***www.thewisdomcenter.cc***

ORDER FORM THE WISDOM CENTER
(All books paperback unless indicated otherwise.)

Qty	Code	Book Title	USA	Total
	B-01	Wisdom For Winning	$10	
	B-02	Five Steps Out Of Depression	$ 3	
	B-03	The Sex Trap	$ 3	
	B-04	Ten Lies People Believe About Money	$ 3	
	B-05	Finding Your Purpose In Life	$ 3	
	B-06	Creating Tomorrow Through Seed-Faith	$ 3	
	B-07	Battle Techniques For War Weary Saints	$ 3	
	B-08	Enjoying the Winning Life	$ 3	
	B-09	Four Forces/Guarantee Career Success	$ 3	
	B-10	The Bridge Called Divorce	$ 3	
	B-11	Dream Seeds	$ 9	
	B-12	The Ministers Encyclopedia, Vol. 1	$20	
	B-13	Seeds Of Wisdom On Dreams And Goals, Vol. 1	$ 3	
	B-14	Seeds Of Wisdom On Relationships, Vol. 2	$ 3	
	B-15	Seeds Of Wisdom On Miracles, Vol. 3	$ 3	
	B-16	Seeds Of Wisdom On Seed-Faith, Vol. 4	$ 3	
	B-17	Seeds Of Wisdom On Overcoming, Vol. 5	$ 3	
	B-18	Seeds Of Wisdom On Habits, Vol. 6	$ 3	
	B-19	Seeds Of Wisdom On Warfare, Vol. 7	$ 3	
	B-20	Seeds Of Wisdom On Obedience, Vol. 8	$ 3	
	B-21	Seeds Of Wisdom On Adversity, Vol. 9	$ 3	
	B-22	Seeds Of Wisdom On Prosperity, Vol. 10	$ 3	
	B-23	Seeds Of Wisdom On Prayer, Vol. 11	$ 3	
	B-24	Seeds Of Wisdom On Faith-Talk, Vol. 12	$ 3	
	B-25	7 Kinds Of People You Cannot Help	$ 5	
	B-26	The God Book	$10	
	B-27	The Jesus Book	$10	
	B-28	The Blessing Bible	$10	
	B-29	The Survival Bible	$10	
	B-30	The Teens Topical Bible	$ 8	
	B-31	Seeds Of Wisdom Topical Bible	$15	
	B-32	The Ministers Topical Bible	$ 8	
	B-33	The Businessmans Topical Bible	$ 8	
	B-34	The Grandparents Topical Bible	$ 8	
	B-35	The Fathers Topical Bible	$ 8	
	B-36	The Mothers Topical Bible	$ 8	
	B-37	The New Belivers Topical Bible	$ 8	
	B-38	The Widows Topical Bible	$ 8	
	B-39	The Double Diamond Principle	$ 9	
	B-40	Wisdom For Crisis Times	$ 9	
	B-41	The Gift Of Wisdom, Vol. 1	$10	
	B-42	One-Minute Businessmans Devotional	$12	
	B-43	One-Minute Businesswomans Devotional	$12	
	B-44	31 Secrets For Career Success	$10	
	B-45	101 Wisdom Keys	$ 5	
	B-46	31 Facts About Wisdom	$ 5	
	B-47	The Covenant Of The Fifty-Eight Blessings	$ 8	
	B-48	31 Keys To A New Beginning	$ 5	
	B-49	The Proverbs 31 Woman	$ 7	
	B-50	One-Minute Pocket Bible for the Achiever	$ 5	
	B-51	One-Minute Pocket Bible for Fathers	$ 5	
	B-52	One-Minute Pocket Bible for Mothers	$ 5	
	B-53	One-Minute Pocket Bible for Teenagers	$ 5	
	B-54	The Seeds Of Wisdom Daily Devotional	$ 5	
	B-55	20 Keys To A Happier Marriage	$ 3	
	B-56	How To Turn Mistakes Into Miracles	$ 3	

Qty	Code	Book Title	USA	Total
	B-57	31 Secrets Of An Unforgettable Woman	$ 9	
	B-58	The Mentors Manna on Attitude	$ 3	
	B-59	The Making Of A Champion	$ 8	
	B-60	One-Minute Pocket Bible For Men	$ 5	
	B-61	One-Minute Pocket Bible For Women	$ 5	
	B-62	One-Minute Pocket Bible/Bus.Professionals	$ 5	
	B-63	One-Minute Pocket Bible For Truckers	$ 5	
	B-64	Seven Obstacles To Abundant Success	$ 3	
	B-65	Born To Taste The Grapes	$ 3	
	B-66	Greed, Gold And Giving	$ 3	
	B-67	Gift Of Wisdom For Champions	$10	
	B-68	Gift Of Wisdom For Achievers	$10	
	B-69	Wisdom Keys For A Powerful Prayer Life	$ 3	
	B-70	Gift of Wisdom For Mothers	$10	
	B-71	Wisdom - God's Golden Key To Success	$ 7	
	B-72	The Double Diamond Daily Devotional	$15	
	B-73	The Mentors Manna On Abilities	$ 3	
	B-74	The Assignment: Dream/Destiny, Vol. 1	$10	
	B-75	The Assignment: Anointing/Adversity, Vol. 2	$10	
	B-76	The Mentors Manna on Assignment	$ 3	
	B-77	The Gift of Wisdom for Fathers	$10	
	B-78	The Mentors Manna on the Secret Place	$ 3	
	B-79	The Mentors Manna on Achievement	$ 3	
	B-80	The Greatest Success Habit on Earth	$ 3	
	B-81	The Mentors Manna on Adversity	$ 3	
	B-82	31 Reasons People Do Not Receive Their Financial Harvest	$12	
	B-83	The Gift Of Wisdom For Wives	$10	
	B-84	The Gift Of Wisdom For Husbands	$10	
	B-85	The Gift Of Wisdom For Teenagers	$10	
	B-86	The Gift Of Wisdom For Leaders	$10	
	B-87	The Gift Of Wisdom For Graduates	$10	
	B-88	The Gift Of Wisdom For Brides	$10	
	B-89	The Gift Of Wisdom For Grooms	$10	
	B-90	The Gift Of Wisdom For Ministers	$10	
	B-91	The Leadership Secrets Of Jesus	$10	
	B-92	Secrets Of The Journey, Vol. 1	$ 5	
	B-93	Secrets Of The Journey, Vol. 2	$ 5	
	B-94	Secrets Of The Journey, Vol. 3	$ 5	
	B-95	Secrets Of The Journey, Vol. 4	$ 5	
	B-96	Secrets Of The Journey, Vol. 5	$ 5	
	B-97	The Assignment: Trials/Triumphs, Vol. 3	$ 5	
	B-98	The Assignment: Pain/Passion, Vol. 4	$ 5	
	B-99	Secrets Of The Richest Man Who Ever Lived	$10	
	B-100	The Holy Spirit Handbook, Vol. 1	$10	
	B-101	The 3 Most Important Things In Your Life	$10	
	B-102	Secrets Of The Journey, Vol. 6	$ 5	
	B-103	Secrets Of The Journey, Vol. 7	$ 5	
	B-104	7 Days To 1000 Times More	$10	
	B-105	31 Days To Succeeding On Your Job	$10	
	B-106	The Uncommon Leader	$ 5	
	B-107	The Uncommon Minister, Vol. 1	$ 5	
	B-108	The Uncommon Minister, Vol. 2	$ 5	
	B-109	The Uncommon Minister, Vol. 3	$ 5	
	B-110	The Uncommon Minister, Vol. 4	$ 5	
	B-111	The Uncommon Minister, Vol. 5	$ 5	
	B-112	The Uncommon Minister, Vol. 6	$ 5	
	B-113	The Uncommon Minister, Vol. 7	$ 5	

Qty	Code	Book Title	USA	Total
	B-114	THE LAW OF RECOGNITION	$10	
	B-115	SEEDS OF WISDOM ON THE SECRET PLACE, VOL. 13	$ 5	
	B-116	SEEDS OF WISDOM ON THE HOLY SPIRIT, VOL. 14	$ 5	
	B-117	SEEDS OF WISDOM ON THE WORD OF GOD, VOL. 15	$ 5	
	B-118	SEEDS OF WISDOM ON PROBLEM SOLVING, VOL. 16	$ 5	
	B-119	SEEDS OF WISDOM ON FAVOR, VOL. 17	$ 5	
	B-120	SEEDS OF WISDOM ON HEALING, VOL. 18	$ 5	
	B-121	SEEDS OF WISDOM ON TIME-MANAGEMENT, VOL. 19	$ 5	
	B-122	SEEDS OF WISDOM ON YOUR ASSIGNMENT, VOL. 20	$ 5	
	B-123	SEEDS OF WISDOM ON FINANCIAL BREAKTHROUGH, VOL. 21	$ 5	
	B-124	SEEDS OF WISDOM ON ENEMIES, VOL. 22	$ 5	
	B-125	SEEDS OF WISDOM ON DECISION-MAKING, VOL. 23	$ 5	
	B-126	SEEDS OF WISDOM ON MENTORSHIP VOL. 24	$ 5	
	B-127	SEEDS OF WISDOM ON GOAL-SETTING, VOL. 25	$ 5	
	B-128	SEEDS OF WISDOM ON THE POWER OF WORDS, VOL. 26	$ 5	
	B-129	THE SECRET OF THE SEED	$10	
	B-130	THE UNCOMMON MILLIONAIRE, VOL. 1	$10	
	B-131	THE UNCOMMON FATHER	$ 8	
	B-132	THE UNCOMMON MOTHER	$ 8	
	B-133	THE UNCOMMON ACHIEVER	$10	
	B-134	THE UNCOMMON ARMORBEARER	$10	
	B-135	THE UNCOMMON DREAM, VOL. 1	$10	
	B-136	THE WISDOM COMMENTARY, VOL 1 (SEED-GIFT)	$100	
	B-137	SEEDOS OF WISDOM ON PRODUCTIVITY	$ 5	
	B-138	SERVICEMAN'S TOPICAL BIBLE	$ 8	
	B-139	TRAVELERS TOPICAL BIBLE	$ 8	
	B-140	31 SCRIPTURES EVERY CHILD SHOULD MEMORIZE	$ 5	
	B-141	31 GREATEST CHAPTERS IN THE BIBLE	$ 8	

☐ CASH ☐ CHECK ☐ MONEY ORDER ☐ VISA	TOTAL PAGES 1, 2, 3	$
CREDIT CARD # ☐ MC ☐ DISCOVER ☐ AMEX	SHIPPING ADD 10%-USA/20%-OTHERS	$
	CANADA CURRENCY DIFFERENCE ADD 20%	$
EXPIRATION DATE ☐☐☐☐ *SORRY NO C.O.D.'s*		
SIGNATURE	TOTAL ENCLOSED	$

PLEASE PRINT

Name_____

Address_____

City_____ State _____ Zip _____

Phone (_____) -_____

E-mail_____

Mail to: **The Wisdom Center** • P.O. Box 99 • Denton, TX 76202
1-888-WISDOM-1 (1-888-947-3661) • Website: **thewisdomcenter.cc**